Involving Parents through Children's Literature
Grades 1-2

Anthony D. Fredericks
Assistant Professor of Education
York College
York, Pennsylvania

Illustrated by
Anthony Allan Stoner

Teacher Ideas Press
An Imprint of Greenwood Publishing Group
361 Hanover Street
Portsmouth, New Hampshire
1992

*To Russ Walsh—whose inspiration I respect,
encouragement I treasure, and friendship I value...
may they always remain constants!*

TEACHER IDEAS PRESS
An Imprint of Greenwood Publishing Group
361 Hanover Street
Portsmouth, NH 03801
1-800-225-5800
www.teacherideaspress.com

Library of Congress Cataloging-in-Publication Data

Fredericks, Anthony D.
    Involving parents through children's literature, grades 1-2 /
Anthony D. Fredericks ; illustrated by Anthony Allan Stoner.
    xxi, 95 p. 22x28 cm.
    Includes index.
    ISBN 1-56308-012-5
    1. Children--Books and reading.   2. Children's literature-
-Appreciation--Problems, exercises, etc.   3. Libraries, Children's-
-Activity programs.   4. Reading--Parent participation. I. Title.
Z1037.A1F74   1992
011.62--dc20   92-13415
                                                           CIP

Docutech RRD 2004

Contents

Acknowledgments

A writer and a word processor are only part of a published work. I am fortunate to have been influenced by many people in the creation of this book. They are the inspiration and the support system for the ideas contained within these pages.

The greatest accolades go to a delightfully talented and tremendously gifted group of preservice teachers at York College who worked closely with me on this project: Stephanie King, Mitzi Karr, Pat Vanderberg, and Stephanie Wilt. Their commitment to a literature-rich environment and their remarkable creative spirit are woven into this book. It is certain that their future classrooms will be filled with books and will overflow with love and laughter.

To Michalene Dauplaise, who spent long hours typing portions of this manuscript, go lots of "warm fuzzies" (and a few hugs). Her unfailing humor and warmth make the Education Department office a joyful workplace.

To my friend and good buddy Russ Walsh goes my undying appreciation for sharing his beautiful and wonderfully inspiring poem. May others be equally touched by his words.

My friends at Libraries Unlimited—Suzanne, David, and Debby—deserve a standing ovation for their continued support and camaraderie. It is truly a professional honor to be able to work with them.

A special commendation award goes to Pat Broderick and Allan Raymond at *TEACHING Pre-K-8* who have supported my monthly column ("Talking to Parents") for a decade. They have been both editors and friends and continue to produce the finest professional magazine around.

Tony Stoner receives a tremendous round of applause for his creative and dynamic illustrations. This book, and the others in the series, are enhanced by his vision and talent.

To all my colleagues on the Parents and Reading Committee and the Parental Involvement Special Interest Group—both part of the International Reading Association—I owe an eternal debt of gratitude for their continued encouragement and inspiration. May their work and vision be reflected in the pages of this book!

Introduction

When I was growing up in southern California, my father and I would take an annual fishing trip up into the High Sierras. Each August, we would pack up the car with camping equipment and fishing paraphernalia and head north out of Los Angeles on Highway 14. We would drive through the heat of the desert past the towns of Palmdale, Lancaster, and Mojave. At Walker Pass we would turn onto Route 395 and begin our ascent into the cool mountains of eastern California. This part of our journey took us through the poetic towns of Little Lake, Olancha, Lone Pine, Independence, Big Pine, and Bishop. A long day of driving later we would eventually arrive at Mammoth Lakes and the Mammoth Lakes Pack Station. We would take a cabin for the night, and that is when it would start.

You see, my father and I had a tradition on our yearly camping trips. We called it "The Impossible Story." The rules were always the same, but the stories were always different. The design was for one of us to begin telling a story with a brave and dashing hero as the central figure (Jack Armstrong was frequently used). The intent was to create a set of circumstances from which it was virtually impossible for the hero to escape and then turn the telling of the story over to the other person. It was that person's task to extricate the hero from that impossible set of circumstances and then put him in another set of seemingly more impossible circumstances from which the other storyteller would have to devise an escape. (I have this theory that the producers of the *Mission Impossible* and *MacGyver* television shows got some of their ideas from our impossible stories.) Here is an abbreviated sampling of a story we may have shared one August night in the mountains of California.

Dad: "Jack Armstrong was a pilot for an air transport company in Alaska. One day, while flying over the Arctic Circle, he noticed that he was low on gas. It was apparent that someone had sabotaged the plane; but there was no time to think about that because the plane had started a long slow dive toward the Arctic Ocean, an ocean inhabited by hungry sharks. Suddenly the fuel line ruptured and the tail of the plane burst into flames. Jack realized he was going to crash into the cold, numbing waters of the sea below. Smoke began to billow into the interior of the plane, making him dizzy and forcing him to lose control. The sharks circled below, the sea was unbelievably cold, and Jack was quickly losing consciousness." O.K. son, now the story is yours.

Me: "Jack crawled into the rear of the plane and quickly saw that the cargo consisted of thousands of handkerchiefs. Suddenly, he got an idea. Working quickly, he began tying the handkerchiefs together, and seconds before the plane crashed into the sea he was able to parachute to safety on a nearby deserted island. But then he realized that he had no supplies and the frigid Arctic night was coming on. Suddenly, he felt a shaking beneath his feet. Looking down, he saw that he was standing on the edge of an enormous volcano that was ready to erupt. The violent shaking knocked him into the mouth of the volcano and he broke both of his legs and one arm in the fall. There was no way he could crawl to safety and he knew the volcano was set to explode within minutes." O.K., Dad, it's your turn.

The story never ended; after 14 days it was just put on hold until the next summer, when it would start all over again.

Those times were very important for me and my father. It was not only a valuable opportunity to get to know each other better but also a time to share the magic of stories and to explore the outer reaches of creativity and inventiveness. We never knew how our stories were going to turn out or where they would take us, but that really did not matter. What did matter was that we could enjoy some make-believe and fantasy and, most important, each other's company.

Much of what I have been able to share with students and other educators has been a direct result of those fishing trips in the High Sierras. My father taught me that education can take place far beyond the walls of a classroom and does not have to be confined to textbooks and worksheets. He also taught me that the most important kind of education is the kind that takes place between parents and their children. Perhaps because my father shared the magic of stories, I am one of those who contend that parents are a child's first and most important teachers.

Involving Parents through Children's Literature grew out of a perceived need to help parents take an active role in their children's reading growth and development. It evolved out of conversations with educators from around the country, workshops with parents in many states, and an investigation of the research supporting the influence parents have on children's education. What surfaced was a desire for parents and children to effect strong interactive bonds via children's literature. In short, reading with one's child is recognized by educators and parents alike as a natural and fundamentally sound way of ensuring reading success. Thus, this book is designed to offer parents, teachers, librarians, and administrators a participatory approach to the dissemination of, and involvement in, good children's books. That is to say, when parents know what books are most appropriate for their children's age and grade level, and are provided with relevant ways to share those recommended books, then reading and learning becomes much more meaningful in a child's life.

While preparing this book, I often heard the questions: "What books are appropriate for my child's age level?" "Are there any lists I can share with parents on suggested books for this grade?" and "How can we as parents become more actively involved in our children's reading growth?" I discovered scores of photocopied lists of recommended books being sent home to parents in a host of schools; a variety of newsletters of every shape, size, and dimension being used to establish communication bonds between schools and homes; and assorted seminars, workshops, and parent/teacher meetings being held throughout the school year. It became obvious that sincere and dedicated efforts were being made to establish a meaningful home-school connection by educators and their schools. It became equally obvious that teachers, librarians, and parents were looking for a coordinated, systematic, and easy-to-implement project that would identify and explore quality children's literature in the home.

This book is based on the idea that when parents know the books they can share with their youngsters as well as the activities that promote an involvement in, and appreciation of, quality literature, then positive literacy development is ensured. This book is also founded on the idea that parents should be involved in helping their children over an extended period of time—the entire school year, for example. In this way, parents and children get a sense that reading and the support of reading is an ongoing effort. The emphasis here is on helping parents demonstrate all the magic, creativity, and imagination that can be shared and enjoyed in books.

HOW TO USE THIS BOOK

This book is designed to help teachers build a lasting and enthusiastic relationship with parents and to help parents extend the learning opportunities of their children through a literate environment. Encouraging parents to become supporters of their children's literacy growth and development can be one of the most important tasks you undertake.

Book Selection

There are hundreds of thousands of children's books available, and more than 5,000 new children's books are published each year. No book of this size could begin to address all the available literature. My choices were based on a combination of the following consultations and considerations:

1. Children's librarians in both public schools and public libraries were consulted on their recommendations of the most appropriate children's literature for the designated grade range. Books checked out of school and public libraries in many parts of the country, as well as librarians' personal choices, were considered.

2. Teachers and reading specialists were also asked to share their ideas on the books that engender positive responses from their students and that provide opportunities for parents and children to share those books through cooperative activities. Also consulted were annual editions of *Teachers' Choices*, an annotated list of new children's trade books for children and adolescents that teachers throughout the country find to be exceptional. (Single copies of each year's list are available free for a self-addressed, 9"-x-12" envelope stamped with first-class postage for 2 ounces. Write to the International Reading Association, 800 Barksdale Road, P.O. Box 8139, Newark, DE 19714-8139.)

3. Students at the designated grade levels were also involved in the selection process. I try to keep an open ear to the kinds of books kids talk about most. I also used books suggested in several editions of *Children's Choices*, an annual compilation of favorite books as designated by school children throughout the United States. (Free copies of each year's edition of *Children's Choices* are available through the International Reading Association. See item 2, above for the address.) Another valuable resource was the *Young Adults' Choices*, an annual collection of popular books as determined by students in middle, junior, and high schools around the United States. (A free copy can be obtained through the International Reading Association.)

4. Award-winning children's literature was also considered in compiling the lists of books. Included are Caldecott Medal and Honor Award books, the Newbery Medal and Honor Award books, Children's Book Award books, American Library Association Notable Books for Children, Reading Rainbow Feature books, and Boston Globe/Horn Book Awards.

5. Books were selected because they were valuable as standards of high-quality children's literature and were also important in promoting literature-related experiences. Books selected represented a cross-section of children's literature, including different genres (fantasy, science fiction, historical fiction, informational, biographies, etc.), social and multicultural experiences, and literary elements (theme, plot, point of view, characterization, and setting).

6. All of the books are those that can extend and enhance children's language development. Through these books, children can examine and explore the world around them, as well as engage in meaningful language-rich experiences with their parents. So too does this collection of books introduce children to their rich literary heritage—there are "classics" as well as newer books in this compilation.

7. Selected books are easily accessible by parents in any school or public library. The literature selections are also those that could be part of family libraries.

8. Finally, the books were chosen for their entertainment and enjoyment value. The intent was to cater to children's interests as well as create interest in new topics (Norton 1991). Some books may be familiar to students; others may not. However, the overall intent is that children will receive a balanced approach to books and reading that can serve as a foundation for a lifetime of reading pleasure.

In the appendix is a list of 99 additional children's books for these grades; this list can be duplicated and sent home. The books on the list are in addition to the 40 books detailed in the main body of this book and meet the same criteria. Thus, you have a total of 139 recommended books for parents and children to enjoy together.

Important Features

Involving Parents through Children's Literature has several features of particular interest to the classroom teacher, reading specialist, school or public librarian, Chapter I teacher, or district administrator:

1. This book contains activity pages for 40 children's literature selections. These pages are designed to be duplicated and sent home with students, perhaps as often as once a week. All the activity pages are set up in the same fashion, as follows:

   a. Bibliographic information (including title, author, and publisher) is provided.

   b. The book is briefly summarized.

   c. Discussion questions are suggested that parents and children can share while or after reading the story. The intent is not to have parents ask all of the questions presented, but rather to give them discussion ideas.

   d. Activities are provided so that parents and children can work together on some extensions of the book that are in keeping with the ability and interests of individual children.

   e. Most of the activity pages also include other books for children and parents to enjoy together. These include books on the same theme as the target book or books written by the same author. One alternative for parents is to read other suggested books with their children.

   f. Included for some of the books, in addition to the activity pages, is a project sheet, which suggests a more open-ended activity that parents and children can work on together. It is important to note that there are no right or wrong answers in any of these activities; rather, parents and students should work together to arrive at mutually satisfying responses.

2. There is no prescribed sequence for sending the activity pages home. You should feel free to distribute them in whatever order you wish. Most teachers will probably elect to send them home in random order, although it is possible to coordinate certain literature selections with particular elements of the reading/language arts curriculum. As you will note, the literature selections have been arranged alphabetically and not by any distribution sequence or level of difficulty.

3. While you are encouraged to use as many (or as few) of the activity pages as you deem appropriate, you are also encouraged to use activities from any of the other three books in the series. If you are a Chapter I teacher or a teacher of the gifted and talented, you may choose more appropriate literature selections from any other book in this series.

4. The activity pages are designed to offer parents and children a variety of relaxing, non-threatening, and supportive activities. While it is certainly important for parents to read to their children on a regular basis, it is equally important that parents and children have sufficient opportunities to discuss books and work together in learning activities that bring literature to life and make books an important part of all students' lives. Thus, there are no tests to give, no "checking up" to do, and no grades to assign. These activities are designed not as homework assignments, but as extensions of the reading program. You should be under no obligation to follow through on whether each family has completed a requisite number of activities for each book. Busy schedules and hectic weeks may preclude some families from doing the suggested activities for a particular book. That is okay! Parents should not feel any obligation to tackle any particular book and its accompanying activities. It would certainly be appropriate for you to suggest that parents obtain a three-ring binder in which they can keep the activity pages for future reference and use. In that way, families will be able to share a specific book and its accompanying activities at a convenient time in their busy schedules.

There are many ways to distribute the activity pages duplicated on one or two sides of a single sheet of paper. You should choose the approach or combination of approaches most appropriate for your classroom and local community. Following are several possibilities for you to consider.

1. Duplicate the activity pages on one or more sheets of paper. Send them home with your students once a week. Designate one day of the week (Friday or Tuesday, for example) as a literature day. By selecting a specific day of the week, parents come to expect the activity pages and may be able to schedule time to pursue the designated activities with their children.

2. Take some time before distributing activity pages to talk about the book with your students. Introduce the book, author, and illustrator, provide an appropriate overview of the plot and theme, and suggest some of the possible activities children and their parents may pursue. You may designate a specific time of the week or month as a Sharing Day, when children tell about some of the activities that they and their parents shared for specific books and some of the things they talked about. Be careful, however, that those students who choose not to actively participate (or who are unable to) are not penalized for their nonparticipation.

3. Feel free to add activities or ideas as you see fit. This will allow you to personalize activity pages according to the specific needs of an individual child. This also sends a signal to parents that you are willing to do more than just send photocopied activity pages to them once each week; rather, you are interested in providing them with ideas that are tailored specifically for their child.

4. It is important for you to mail an introductory letter (see the appendix, pages 75, 76, and 79) to parents before sending any of the subsequent activity pages. This letter provides parents with valuable information on the dynamics of your program and the role(s) they are expected to play. Although you may want to send the activity pages home with students, consider mailing them instead (you may be able to do this through the principal's office, the district office, or the local parent-teacher organization).

5. Consider sending the activity pages in packets. Although these are designed to be sent home weekly, consider other alternatives. For example, you may decide to send home activity pages for two books every two weeks or for four books every month. Such an option allows you (and, of course, parents) more opportunities to introduce books and children more opportunities to read books independently and pursue suggested activities in more detail.

6. It is not important for all students to receive the same activity pages at the same time (this may cause a "run" on the school or public library for a specific book). You may want to send different students different activity pages throughout the year. This permits access to as many of the available books as possible. It is advantageous to duplicate as many of the activity pages as possible early in the school year and have them on hand to send home randomly throughout the year.

7. Since many schools send home a periodic newsletter to parents, consider having activity pages attached to the school's newsletter.

8. Call your students' parents to ask if they are receiving the activity pages. Ask how they are enjoying sharing the activities with their children. This also provides you with an opportunity to recommend other books and other activities for parents and children to pursue together.

9. Ask your building principal to write a letter to parents that mentions the importance of these activity pages and reasons why parents and children should be sharing books and activities. You may be able to enlist the aid of a supervisor or the district superintendent to create an appropriate letter for distribution to parents, too.

10. Make sure that any special functions at school (e.g., a meet-the-teacher night, an open house, book fairs, and parent/teacher conferences) include information on the activity pages. Samples of the activity pages and descriptive information can be easily distributed to all the parents in your classroom or at a specific grade level during these special meetings.

11. Encourage your students to suggest alternate ways to distribute activity pages to parents. Students may wish to consider some of the following distribution methods as possibilities:

    a. Record activities on cassette tape, make copies, and distribute to parents.

    b. Have the activity pages sent out through a local community agency: YMCA, Boy's Club, Little League, or day camp.

    c. Have the activity pages distributed through a fraternal organization: Moose, Elks, Rotary, Knights of Columbus, etc.

    d. Have the activity pages duplicated and available for pick up at any one of several local public libraries.

    e. Have portions of an activity page duplicated and included in newsletters distributed by local clubs, organizations, or religious groups.

    f. Post samples of activity pages on community bulletin boards.

    g. Record activity pages on the school's answering machine and encourage parents to call in regularly.

12. Keep promoting the activity pages in whatever communications you have with parents. Phone calls, meetings, conferences, notes, and the like can all be vehicles for disseminating information about their usefulness.

PROMOTING THE LITERATURE BOND

What follows is a list of suggestions you may wish to consider in promoting literature to the families of all the students in your classroom. This is not intended as a complete list, but rather one that will stimulate the creation of additional ideas for promoting literature bonds between parents and children. You are certainly encouraged to revise and modify these suggestions in terms of the dynamics of your own classroom or community. However, it will be vitally important that you maintain a regular system of promotion efforts throughout the school year. This alerts parents to the notion that books and literature are a vital part of both the school curriculum and the "home curriculum."

- Set up special literature workshops for parents. These once-a-month meetings can present new children's books and the accompanying activities and projects parents and children can do together to extend literature in the home.

- Prepare public service announcements on the value of parents and children reading books together. Distribute these to local radio stations.

- Prepare stories or messages to be placed on the telephone answering machine of the school or district office. Included could be recommended children's literature and one or two accompanying activities.

- Prepare special brochures, flyers, or leaflets on selected children's books (students can work along with teachers in designing these). Send these home to parents periodically.

- Write a letter to the editor of the local newspaper on the value of parents and children reading together. Offer a bibliography of selected children's books for interested readers.

- Invite parents to visit your classroom on a regular basis to read selected books to all members of the class.

- Hold a monthly Parent Tea to share ideas and discuss new books added to the school or classroom library.

- Ask the district superintendent to prepare a letter (to be sent to the parents of your students) on the value of reading in the home.

- Set up a "telephone tree," a system by which parents of students in your classroom can call other parents to relay news about children's books and to suggest some activities to use with those books.

- Invite parents to participate on a Literature Council to help select new books for the classroom or school library.

- Call two parents each week to share some information about one or more children's books.

- Have students write generic letters to all the families in your classroom. These letters could suggest popular or new books for families to share together and include ideas for hands-on activities that the students themselves generate.

- Invite parents to participate in a Family Reading Night, an evening in which parents and children gather to share favorite stories and related activities.

- Encourage parents to participate continuously throughout the education of their children. Effective programs are built up over time and should not be viewed as one-shot affairs but as a lifelong commitment.

- Act as good role models for parents. That is, be enthusiastic and committed to the idea of a literature-based reading experience for all students.

- Have your students design contemporary cards based on several selected books. The front of each card can have an illustration from a book, along with bibliographic information. The inside of each card can have one or two extending activities for family use. These cards can be prepared and mailed to families throughout the year.

- Be sure to include a note about new children's books or popular children's literature when sending out report cards.

- Send personal invitations to parents to bring a brown bag lunch and spend a lunch period with your class. This time can be used for the sharing of selected books by individuals or small groups.

- Set up a Book of the Week or Author of the Month program and disseminate information to parents in the form of a monthly newsletter.

- Set up a series of home visits to meet with families in their homes if possible. Take along a selection of relevant children's literature and share these books with parents.

- Direct your students to prepare a series of posters promoting popular books. Distribute these posters around town (the bank, post office, hardware store, etc.). Replace the posters monthly.

- Provide opportunities for parents and children to work together on selected literature-based activities. A monthly meeting of parents and children from several different classrooms could be coordinated by several teachers working together.

- Get all family members involved in outreach efforts. Grandparents, siblings, and extended family members can participate in a literature-based home reading project.

- Continually seek the involvement of all families. Give everyone a chance to participate. Make your outreach efforts contagious.

- Provide parents with a list of bookstores or teacher supply stores in your local area (some parents may not be aware of where they can purchase children's literature). Also, be sure to provide a list of libraries in your area and their hours of operation.

- Establish a series of "make-and-take" workshops in which parents can create learning materials related to selected children's books. These materials can then be distributed to other parents in the classroom or throughout the school.

- Encourage parents to get library cards for each member of the family. You may wish to contact your local public library to obtain the necessary forms, which may be sent home with students.

- Be sure to talk with parents about appropriate children's books during regularly scheduled parent/teacher conferences. You may wish to prepare a list of suggested books for distribution at the conferences.

- Establish a Parent Responsibility contract to be signed at the beginning of the year. The contract should be designed to encourage a regular reading time between students and parents (e.g., from 7:30 to 8:00 each evening).

- Keep tabs on upcoming TV shows and movies, many of which are based on children's books. Check your local video store for movie versions of children's books and provide a list of these to parents (watching a video version of a book may encourage the reading of the original).

- Always let parents know that you are proud to have them as partners in all your literacy efforts.

- Work along with your local public librarian and prepare lists of upcoming events at the library. Distribute the lists to families on a regular basis.

- Interview various groups of students about some of their favorite books. Prepare a list of these books and distribute it to your students' families.

- Set up a Family Book of the Month club and provide opportunities for families to share some of the books and stories they read at home. This can be done through a periodic newsletter sent to all families.

- Invite the mayor of your city or town to issue a Families Reading Together proclamation (a simple request on school letterhead is often all that is needed).

- Invite youngsters to design and create a parent involvement or literature logo that can be used on all outgoing messages and newsletters.

- Set up a classroom quiz show in which families compete on their knowledge of selected children's books (a sort of "Literature Family Feud").

- Invite students to send a letter or note to the parents of fellow students telling them why they should read a particular book. Make this a regular activity (once a month, for example).

- Prepare a list of recommended books to give to the parents of new students transferring into your classroom. A collection of some of the handouts from this book would also be an appropriate welcome for new students.

- Establish a Grandparents Club in which grandparents or other senior citizens visit your classroom to share favorite children's books. Take photographs and have students conduct interviews and prepare news stories for inclusion in a monthly newsletter.

- Set up an exhibit in a local shopping mall that would include photos of parents and children reading together, tips on parent participation, lists of recommended books for selected grade levels, and other home reading activities.

- Work with a group of students and/or parents to develop a slide/tape program of suggested children's books. The slides could be distributed to all parents through a library checkout system.

- Work with a local college's education department to set up special parent programs on the use of children's literature in the home and the value of parents and youngsters reading together.

- Read a portion of a children's book to all the students in your classroom. Encourage parents to obtain the book (through the local library or bookstore) and complete the reading of the story at home.

- Prepare a series of brief notes that can be duplicated and attached to homework papers throughout the school year. Each note can contain one or two recommendations for children's books and some selected discussion questions or extending activities. Keep these notes brief and send them home regularly throughout the year.

- Take time periodically to write a letter to selected parents recommending books for their children. Be aware of students' interests and suggest literature in keeping with those interests.

- Work with your students in designing a series of special certificates or awards that can be sent home to parents periodically. These awards can be given to recognize parents who share good literature with their children (be careful, however; the awards should *not* be given for completing a specified number of activities).

- Prepare a checklist of things parents should be doing at home with their children to promote good books and good reading habits. An appropriate one can be found in *Letters to Parents* by Anthony D. Fredericks and Elaine P. LeBlanc (Glenview, IL: Scott, Foresman, 1986).

- Have your students set up a "recruiting office." Solicit ideas and suggestions from class members on how to fully involve all families in a literature-based reading program. What types of activities do your students think might encourage parents and children to share more books? Collect their ideas and distribute them through a periodic newsletter.

- Work with a local public librarian to establish a series of Saturday Morning Book Talks. Each regularly scheduled book talk could introduce parents to some of the latest in children's literature as well as some extending activities families could share at home.

- Prepare videotapes of current books and selected activities to be used with the books (you've probably got a classroom full of natural actors). Make these videos available to parents.

As you use this book, please feel free to modify or alter activities and suggestions in keeping with the abilities of your students and the dynamics of your classroom. It is also important for you to solicit the input of parents as to how these activity pages are being used and how they can be improved. Providing opportunities for parents to "buy into" these activities will give them a sense of ownership that will result in heightened levels of participation. These activities achieve their greatest impact when parents know that their insights and feedback are solicited and valued. You will discover those insights useful in future years.

I sincerely hope you find these materials to be an appropriate means of communicating with parents about good books and good reading habits. Also, I hope you discover that when parents are actively involved in the dynamics of your reading program, anything is possible.

Anthony D. Fredericks

Books and Activities

Read to Me, Daddy

Read to me, Daddy
Of far away places
Where elephants reign
And turtles win races.

Read to me, Daddy
And we'll leave on a flight
To Jupiter! Mars!
And home in one night.

Read to me, Daddy
And fill up my head
With fanciful pictures
'Fore I go to bed.

Read to me, Daddy
Of wishes come true.
Read to me, Daddy
Then I'll read to you.

Russ Walsh, 1986

Albert's Toothache
Barbara Williams
(New York: E. P. Dutton, 1974)

STORY SUMMARY

Albert says he has a toothache and no one in his family believes him because turtles do not have teeth. It takes a caring grandmother to find out what Albert's problem really is.

DISCUSSION QUESTIONS

1. How would you feel if you were telling the truth and no one believed you?

2. What do you think would have happened to Albert if his grandmother had not come to visit?

3. Why do you think Albert called his hurt toe a toothache?

4. How do you think the story would have been different if turtles had teeth?

5. Would you tell a friend about this book? Why?

6. If you could be any character in this book, which one would you like to be? Why?

ACTIVITIES (Please choose any two activities.)

1. You may enjoy reading other books about turtles. Here are some you may want to check out of your local public library: *Timothy Turtle* by Al Green, *Turtles* by Janet Craig, *What Is a Turtle?* by Gene Darby, and *When Turtle Come to Town* by Cary B. Ziter.

2. Have your child suggest ways the family's life would be different if, like turtles, no one had teeth. Record your child's ideas. Prepare a meal that does not require any chewing (baby food could be used). Discuss how a "chewless" meal feels.

3. You could plan to have a turtle party with "turtle foods" suggested in the book:
   - gummy worms...green caterpillars
   - black licorice...gray spider legs
   - sunflower seeds..sunflower seeds
   - raisins..rotten oak bark
   - parsley .... leaves

4. Design a publicity poster for the book. Have your child use construction paper, markers, and crayons, to design an "advertisement" for the book. Hang the completed poster in the living room or on the refrigerator door.

5. Visit a local pet shop to observe any turtles on display. Talk together about some of the features seen on the turtles. If possible, purchase a turtle as a pet. If not, develop together a brochure on the care and feeding of turtles.

6. Your child may enjoy making finger puppets of some of the characters from the book. The fingers from several old gloves can be cut off and decorated with markers, yarn, buttons, etc. Put on one or more finger puppets and re-create favorite portions of the book together.

7. Your child may enjoy listening to several turtle poems from *The Random House Book of Poetry for Children* by Jack Prelutsky (New York: Random House, 1983). Here are some suggestions:

    "Desert Tortoise"

    "The First Tooth"

    "Turtle Soup"

8. Work together to create your own poems about turtles. For example:

    Turtles have hard shells
    They move real slow
    I want one as a pet
    But Mom says no!

    Give your child an opportunity to illustrate each poem you create together. Be sure these are posted in an appropriate place for all family members to enjoy.

RELATED CHILDREN'S BOOKS

Grandmother by Jeannie Baker
Grandma Is Somebody Special by Susan Goldman
Turtle Pond by Berniece Freschet
Arthur's Tooth by Marc Brown
My Dentist by Harlow Rockwell
The Random House Book of Poetry for Children by Jack Prelutsky
Move Over, Mother Goose!: Finger Plays, Action Verses and Funny Rhymes by Ruth I. Powell
Fingerpuppets, Fingerplays, and Holidays by Betty Keefe

A Boy, a Dog, a Frog, and a Friend
Mercer Mayer and Marianna Mayer
(New York: The Dial Press, 1971)

STORY SUMMARY

This is the story of a boy, a dog, and a frog on a most adventurous fishing trip. They meet a turtle who causes them quite a bit of trouble. However, in the end they all become friends and travel home together.

DISCUSSION QUESTIONS

1. Why do you think the authors wrote this book without words?

2. Do you think the events of this story could really have taken place?

3. Do you like stories without words? Why or why not?

4. How would you feel if you were the turtle?

5. Which character would you like to be? Why?

ACTIVITIES (Please choose any two activities.)

1. Work with your child to create some words and dialogue for this book. Together write some story events and narration for the characters. If possible, type up the story and include it with the book in the family library.

2. Discuss friendship. What qualities do people look for in a friend? Why are some people our friends and others are not? What does one have to do to be a good friend to someone else? What kinds of things do friends do together?

3. Consider purchasing a special kit that allows your child to raise a frog at home. Two companies that sell these kits are Delta Education (P.O. Box 950, Hudson, NH 03051) and Three Rivers Amphibian, Inc. (P.O. Box 406, Massapequa, NY 11758). Write to them to obtain their latest catalogs (the kits sell for about $15.00 each).

4. Have your child write a thank-you letter to a friend for being so wonderful.

5. If possible, take a trip to a local humane society shelter for animals. Talk about some of the animals and the care necessary for their survival. Upon returning home your child may wish to create a poster of his or her favorite animal.

6. You may enjoy making a collage about boys, dogs, frogs, turtles, and friends. Have your child cut out pictures from several old magazines and paste them on a large sheet of construction paper or newsprint. The completed collage can be displayed in your child's bedroom.

RELATED CHILDREN'S BOOKS

Best Friends by Mariam Cohen
Will I Have a Friend? by Miriam Cohen
Friends by Helme Heine

George and Martha One Fine Day by James Marshall
We Are Best Friends by Aliki
Let's Be Friends Again! by Hans Wilhelm

Bread and Jam for Frances
Russell Hoban
(New York: Harper & Row, 1964)

STORY SUMMARY

Frances enjoys eating bread and jam. She gets upset with her parents when that is all they will feed her.

DISCUSSION QUESTIONS

1. Do you think Frances's parents did the right thing? Why or why not?

2. What might have happened if Frances had continued to eat only one thing?

3. What is your favorite food? Would you be able to eat that food every day for a week? For a month? For a year?

4. What would your friends like most about this book?

5. Does Frances remind you of anybody? If so, who?

ACTIVITIES (Please choose any two activities.)

1. Provide your child with construction paper, scissors, and crayons. Ask your child to create raccoon illustrations of Frances and her family. Cut out the illustrations and paste each of the figures on a separate tongue depressor. You can put on a puppet show of some of the events that take place in the story. If possible, take some photographs of the puppet show and place them in the family album.

2. Have your child write out a procedure for making bread and jam. For example:

   > Take out bread. Take out jam.
   > Lay 2 pieces of bread on plate.
   > Spoon 1 teaspoon full of jam onto 1 piece of bread.
   > Smooth evenly with knife.
   > Put pieces together. Eat!

3. Make some homemade jam together. Here's a simple recipe:

12 ounces dried apricots	5 cups water
20-ounce can pineapple and juice	3½ cups sugar
8-ounce jar maraschino cherries and juice	1 package Sure-Jell™

   Grind the fruit. Add juice and water; let stand 1 hour. Cook 15 minutes and then add sugar. When clear, add Sure-Jell and cook 5 minutes more.

4. Have your child choose favorite foods to eat in place of foods he or she dislikes. If possible, try to have this food available at every meal you serve for at least a week. Discuss together whether too much of a good thing is really not so good.

RELATED CHILDREN'S BOOKS

From Grain to Bread by Ali Mitgutsch
Let's Eat! by True Kelley
Eating by John Gaskin

Project for *Bread and Jam for Frances*

DIRECTIONS

Work with your child to fill in the spaces below. Keep in mind that there are no right or wrong answers. Be sure to talk about reasons why you enjoy some foods and dislike others. Have your child do the same.

FOODS I LIKE

FOODS I DON'T LIKE

_____

_____

_____

_____

_____

_____

FOODS MY PARENT LIKES

FOODS MY PARENT DISLIKES

_____

_____

_____

_____

_____

FOODS _____ LIKES

FOODS _____ DISLIKES

_____

_____

_____

_____

_____

_____

Brown Bear, Brown Bear, What Do You See?
Bill Martin, Jr.
(New York: Henry Holt, 1967)

STORY SUMMARY

This book takes the reader through nine "basic" colors in a rhythmic and enjoyable pattern. The author uses familiar objects that readers can relate to in their own lives.

DISCUSSION QUESTIONS

1. Where are some other places you have seen these colors?

2. What are some other colors that the author did not discuss in the book? Where would they be found?

3. Do you think there is such a thing as a blue horse? Or a purple cat? Why?

4. Are goldfish really made of gold?

5. What are some other colors for bears, frogs, birds, dogs, cats, horses, ducks, fish, and sheep?

ACTIVITIES (Please choose any two activities.)

1. Using the primary colors—red, yellow, and blue—give your child three disposable drinking cups, each filled with a water-based paint of those colors (available at any variety or hobby store). Give your child a small paintbrush, a paper towel, an old shirt (for drips), a cup of clean water, and a sheet of white construction paper. Experiment with mixing the colors to get new colors. (You may want to start by mixing yellow and blue to get green.)

2. Assemble an animal scrapbook. Cut pictures of animals out of old magazines and glue them onto sheets of construction paper. The construction paper can be stapled or sewn along one side to create a "book." Your child may wish to create several books—of land animals, sea animals, and flying animals, for example.

3. Create one or more new stories using this book as an example. Here are some possibilities: "Brown Bear, Brown Bear, What Do You Feel?" "Brown Bear, Brown Bear, What Do You Taste?" "Brown Bear, Brown Bear, What Do You Hear?"

4. Another option would be to create a book using the members of your family. For example, "Mommy, Mommy, What Do You See?"

RELATED CHILDREN'S BOOKS

Tom's Rainbow Walk by Catherine Anhott
Colors by John J. Reiss
...What Do You Hear? by Bill Martin, Jr.
I Never Saw a Purple Cow by Emma Clark
Going Green by John Elkington
Harold and the Purple Crayon by Crockett Johnson
Little Red Hen by Paul Galdone
Mystery of the Blue Paint by Steven Kellogg

Project for *Brown Bear, Brown Bear, What Do You See?*

DIRECTIONS

Work with your child to locate items in your house that are red, blue, green, etc. Afterwards, locate items outside your house that represent each of the listed colors.

	IN THE HOUSE	OUTSIDE THE HOUSE
Red:	_____	_____
	_____	_____
Blue:	_____	_____
	_____	_____
Green:	_____	_____
	_____	_____
Brown:	_____	_____
	_____	_____
Purple:	_____	_____
	_____	_____
Yellow:	_____	_____
	_____	_____
Orange:	_____	_____
	_____	_____
White:	_____	_____
	_____	_____
Black:	_____	_____
	_____	_____

From *Involving Parents through Children's Literature: Grades 1-2*, 1992 • Libraries Unlimited, Inc. • P.O. Box 6633, Englewood, CO 80155-6633

A Chair for My Mother

Vera B. Williams
(New York: Greenwillow Books, 1982)

STORY SUMMARY

A young girl wishes to purchase a chair for her mother, who works hard at a local diner. Although a fire destroys their home, the girl is eventually able to realize her dream.

DISCUSSION QUESTIONS

1. What would you buy with your savings?

2. Why is it important to save for something you really want?

3. How would you feel if you lost all your belongings in a fire?

4. Why is it important to help other people?

5. Why do you think the neighbors wanted to help the family with clothes and furniture?

ACTIVITIES (Please choose any two activities.)

1. Ask your child to draw a picture of his or her favorite chair. Is it a chair in the house, in a furniture store, or in a magazine ad? What makes that chair so special?

2. Have your child write ads, in newspaper format, for a favorite restaurant. It may be helpful for your child to refer to newspaper or magazine ads.

3. Take a trip to a nearby furniture store and have your child test several chairs. Upon your return home, have your child write a brief description of the chair he or she likes the most.

4. Read the story "Goldilocks and the Three Bears" to your child. Talk about the similarities between Goldilocks trying out the chairs in the three bears' house and the family in *A Chair for My Mother* trying out all the chairs in the different furniture stores.

5. Go over the fire exits in your house. Work together to prepare a safety guide for the entire family on what to do in case of a fire. Draw illustrations of exits and write or dictate escape procedures.

RELATED CHILDREN'S BOOKS

Tight Times by Barbara Shook Hazen
My Daddy Don't Go to Work by Madeena Spray Nolan
Benjy Goes to a Restaurant by Jill Krementz
Something Special for Me by Vera B. Williams
Stringbean's Trip to the Shining Sea by Vera B. Williams
Three Days on a River in a Red Canoe by Vera B. Williams

Project for *A Chair for My Mother*

DIRECTIONS

With your child look through the classified advertisements of your local newspaper. Locate ads for furniture and share them with your child. Also, look through the newspaper for advertisements for furniture stores. Share some of those with your child, too. In the spaces below, work with your child to create a classified or display advertisement, or both, for a piece of furniture in your house.

FOR SALE:

_____

_____

_____

_____

_____

_____

_____

*   *   *   *   *   *   *   *   *   *   *   *   *   *   *   *

*   *

*   *

*   *

*   *

*   *

*   *

*   *

*   *

*   *

*   *   *   *   *   *   *   *   *   *   *   *   *   *   *   *

Corduroy
Don Freeman
(New York: Viking Press, 1968)

STORY SUMMARY

Corduroy is a teddy bear who is missing a button on his green corduroy bib-overalls. One day a little girl notices him in the store window and wants to buy him. When she takes him home, he feels as though he is in a palace.

DISCUSSION QUESTIONS

1. Why is Corduroy such a special bear?

2. Why do you think the little girl picked Corduroy over all the other beautiful toys?

3. How do you think Corduroy felt when he left the store?

4. Do you have a toy that is very special to you? Why?

5. Would you have bought Corduroy? Why or why not?

6. What would have happened to Corduroy if the little girl had not found him?

7. Corduroy said he had always wanted to live in a palace. Where would you like to live?

8. If you could be a toy on a shelf, what toy would you want to be and why?

ACTIVITIES (Please choose any two activities.)

1. Take your child on a field trip to a toy store. Talk about what makes some toys more valuable than others (other than price). Help your child understand that cost is not necessarily equivalent to value. On your return home have your child write about what he or she thinks was the most important part of the trip.

2. Locate pictures of teddy bears in magazines or toy catalogs. Have your child cut out several and paste them on a single sheet of construction paper. Provide a title for this collage and post it in his or her bedroom.

3. Have your child write an original story about how Corduroy lost his button. Share the story with other family members.

4. Corduroy got lost in the store. Have your child pretend that he or she brings Corduroy home to your house. Ask your child to draw a map of your house for Corduroy to use so that he will not get lost.

5. You and your child will enjoy reading other Corduroy books such as *Corduroy's Party, A Pocket for Corduroy, Corduroy's Day*, and *Corduroy's Toys*.

6. Have your child draw a map of your town and mark a route showing where he or she would take Corduroy for a day's outing.

7. Create posters saying: "Have You Seen This Bear?" When several posters are completed, post them around the house for a few days.

8. Make bear cookies together. Locate a bear-shaped cookie cutter and use the following recipe.

> 2 cups butter
> 3 cups powdered sugar
> 2 eggs
> 2 teaspoons vanilla
> 5 cups flour
> 2 teaspoons baking soda
> 2 teaspoons cream of tartar
> ½ teaspoon salt

   Cream butter and sugar. Add eggs and vanilla. Mix the dry ingredients and add to creamed mixture. The dough will be stiff. Patiently mix with hands or an electric mixer. Roll the dough to desired thickness. Cut out bear cookies and decorate with colored sugar, raisins, nuts, etc. Bake at 350 degrees for 12-15 minutes.

9. Collect as many different types of buttons as possible (good supplies can be found at local yard sales and thrift stores). Ask your child to sort the buttons into various groupings (by color, size, shape, weight, etc.).

10. Provide samples of various fabrics (cotton, silk, wool, rayon, and, of course, corduroy). Ask your child to describe the similarities and differences among the various fabrics. Glue each piece to a separate sheet of paper and label with its appropriate name and identifying characteristics.

RELATED CHILDREN'S BOOKS

Love Is a Special Way of Feeling by Joan Walsh Anglund
A Very Special Friend by Dorothy Levi
Teach Me about Friends by Joy Berry
Friends by Helen Oxenbury
The Forgotten Bear by Consuelo Joerns
The Secret World of Teddy Bears by Pamela Prince
The Night It Rained Toys by Dorothy Stephenson
Department Store by Gail Gibbons
The Toy Store by Peter Spier
Bear Goes Shopping by Harriet Ziefert

Curious George
H. A. Rey
(Boston: Houghton Mifflin, 1941)

STORY SUMMARY

A man with a yellow hat spies George in an African jungle and decides to bring him back to the United States. George's curiosity gets him into all sorts of exciting adventures.

DISCUSSION QUESTIONS

1. Why are animals kept in zoos?

2. What do you like most about monkeys? What do you like least?

3. How would the story have been different if Curious George had been an elephant? A tiger? A bug?

4. What do you think it would be like to fly on a string of balloons?

5. Would you recommend this book to your friends? Why?

6. Is Curious George similar to anyone you know? If so, who?

ACTIVITIES (Please choose any two activities.)

1. Visit a local travel agency. Ask for several brochures on Africa or any other distant location. Take the brochures home and discuss with your child some of the preparations needed to visit those sites. Have your child prepare a guide on the preparations needed for a trip to Grandmother's (for example) or to a neighborhood store.

2. Ask your child to write a story of what George saw on his balloon ride. Your child may enjoy writing another story about some of the things he or she would enjoy seeing on a balloon trip.

3. Play a game of animal charades. One selects a zoo animal and pantomimes the actions of that animal. The object is for the other to guess the name of the animal. Switch roles.

4. If possible, visit a local fire station and talk with one of the firefighters about fire safety rules. Talk with your child about the need to practice fire safety each and every day.

5. Read other books about Curious George, including *Curious George Rides a Bike, Curious George Takes a Job, Curious George Gets a Medal*, and *Curious George Flies a Kite*.

RELATED CHILDREN'S BOOKS

The Story of the Teasing Monkey by Helen Bannerman
Monkey in the Middle by Eve Bunting
The Monkey and the Crab by Seishi Horio
Oswald, the Monkey by Egon Mathiesen
Monkey in the Jungle by Edna Preston

Project for *Curious George*

DIRECTIONS

Pretend that your child could talk with Curious George. What would he or she like to say to George? How would George answer? Work with your child to create a make-believe dialogue. Write in the questions and the answers Curious George might give.

Your Child: _____

_____

_____

Curious George: _____

_____

_____

Your Child: _____

_____

_____

Curious George: _____

_____

_____

Your Child: _____

_____

_____

Curious George: _____

_____

_____

Your Child: _____

_____

_____

Curious George: _____

_____

From *Involving Parents through Children's Literature: Grades 1-2*, 1992 • Libraries Unlimited, Inc. • P.O. Box 6633, Englewood, CO 80155-6633

Danny and the Dinosaur
Syd Hoff
(New York: Harper & Row, 1958)

STORY SUMMARY

Danny visits the museum and is delighted when one of the dinosaurs comes to life. The two of them spend the rest of the day seeing the city.

DISCUSSION QUESTIONS

1. Do you think the dinosaur would be an interesting friend to have? Why or why not?

2. How would your life be different if dinosaurs were alive today?

3. How do you think people would react if you spent the day going around your town with a dinosaur?

4. Do you think dinosaurs would make good pets? Why or why not?

5. Compare what Danny did with the dinosaur and what you could do with a dog. What is similar and what is different about the two animals?

ACTIVITIES (Please choose any two activities.)

1. Have your child write another version of the story, choosing his or her favorite dinosaur and creating original activities to do if the dinosaur came to life. Post the stories throughout the house.

2. Have your child invent a mythical dinosaur by combining characteristics of known dinosaurs. Draw this new dinosaur and give it a name. Post the illustration on the refrigerator door.

3. Have your child create dinosaur collages by cutting out various pictures of dinosaurs from old magazines and pasting them onto large sheets of construction paper.

4. Buy or make modeling clay (available at any variety or hobby store). Have your child mold new or already known dinosaurs. Work together and write descriptions of the dinosaurs.

5. Invite your child to write about one day in the life of a dinosaur. What things would the dinosaur see, what adventures would the dinosaur experience, and what kinds of food would the dinosaur eat?

6. Take on the roles of two dinosaurs. Conduct a make-believe conversation between the dinosaurs.

RELATED CHILDREN'S BOOKS

Patrick's Dinosaur by Carol Carrick
Digging up Dinosaurs by Aliki
Tyrannosaurus Was a Beast by Jack Prelutsky
Dinosaur Hunt by George Whitaker
Dinosaurs and All That Rubbish by Michael Foreman
Giant Dinosaurs by Erna Rowe

Project for *Danny and the Dinosaur*

DIRECTIONS

A Venn diagram is two overlapping rectangles that show how two or three items are both different and alike. Look at the example below where one rectangle stands for dogs and the other stands for cats. The overlap section in the middle stands for dogs *and* cats.

DOGS	BOTH	CATS
bark	four legs	meow
growl	fur	purr
hate cats	love kids	hate dogs

Work together to complete the following Venn diagram for dinosaurs and a favorite animal (such as a pet). Make a list of things that relate to dinosaurs only, a list that relates to a pet only, and a list that relates to both animals. Try to put five words in each list.

DINOSAUR	DINOSAUR AND PET	PET
_____	_____	_____
_____	_____	_____
_____	_____	_____
_____	_____	_____
_____	_____	_____

The Day Jimmy's Boa Ate the Wash

Trinka Hakes Noble
(New York: Dial Books, 1980)

STORY SUMMARY

A boring class trip to the farm turns into an uproariously funny series of events involving cows, pigs, an egg fight, a busload of kids, and, of course, a boa constrictor.

DISCUSSION QUESTIONS

1. Why wasn't the girl very excited about the class trip?

2. What do you think the farmer and his wife will do with the boa constrictor?

3. What was the funniest part of the story? Why?

4. What do you think Jimmy will do with his new pet pig?

5. Why would your friends enjoy this book?

ACTIVITIES (Please choose any two activities.)

1. Stuff some discarded panty hose or nylon stockings with cloth scraps or crumpled newspaper. Paint a face on one end to turn the stocking into a replica of a boa constrictor. Retell the story while your child manipulates the boa constrictor.

2. Call the biology department of a local college or university and ask if they have any snakes on display. Find out if you and your child can view any snakes and talk with someone about snakes and how they live.

3. Ask your child to dictate or write a story entitled "The Day the Boa Came to Our School."

4. Discuss with your child some of the adventures the boa may have gotten into after the class trip. Later, you may enjoy the sequel to this book entitled *Jimmy's Boa Bounces Back* (New York: Dial Books, 1984).

5. Draw the outlines of several different items of clothing (shirts, pants, shoes, etc.) on pieces of construction paper and cut them out. Tie a piece of string between two places in your child's room. Ask your child to write down one important word from the story on each piece of paper clothing. Use clothespins to clip the words to the string. Occasionally ask your child to use one of the words in an original sentence.

6. You may enjoy reading other books by this author, including *Apple Tree Christmas*, *Hansy's Mermaid*, *The King's Tea*, and *Meanwhile Back at the Ranch*.

RELATED CHILDREN'S BOOKS

Slithers by Syd Hoff	*Crictor* by Tomi Ungerer
To Bathe a Boa by Imbior Kudrna	*The Snake* by Bernard Waber
Snakes Are Hunters by Patricia Lauber	*Python's Party* by Brian Wildsmith

Project for *The Day Jimmy's Boa Ate the Wash*

DIRECTIONS

Help your child use the boxes below to write words or sentences that complete each statement.

If I lived on a farm...

Things I would need:	Things I would miss:

Page 1 of a 2-page handout.

From *Involving Parents through Children's Literature: Grades 1-2*, 1992 • Libraries Unlimited, Inc. • P.O. Box 6633, Englewood, CO 80155-6633

Things I could do:	Things I would never use:

Do You Want to Be My Friend?
Eric Carle
(New York: Harper & Row, 1971)

STORY SUMMARY

This is the story of a little mouse looking for a friend. After asking all the other animals, it finally finds a friend in another mouse.

DISCUSSION QUESTIONS

1. Why wouldn't the other animals be friends with the mouse?

2. Do you think the mouse was lonely? Why or why not?

3. How do you think the mouse felt among the big animals?

4. What would the mouse need to do so that the other animals would be friendly?

ACTIVITIES (Please choose any two activities.)

1. Work with your child to write some words and sentences for the story. What would each of the animals say? What would the mouse say in return?

2. Change the story, putting your child in place of the mouse. What would your child say to each of the animals?

3. Work together and cut out from old magazines several examples of each of the animals mentioned in the story. Paste them on a large sheet of newsprint or construction paper and display the poster.

4. Invite your child to tell you a sequel to the story. What happens to the two mice? What kinds of adventures do they encounter? What will the two of them say to the other animals?

5. Visit a local pet store and examine the mice they have on display. You can purchase or check out from the library a book about caring for rodents (rats and mice). Decide if a mouse would be an appropriate kind of pet for your child to have.

6. Turn an old white sock into a mouse puppet. Draw facial features on the sock and glue on yarn, buttons, and scraps of fabric. Retell the story with your child using the mouse puppet to re-create the action.

7. You may enjoy reading other books by Eric Carle: *The Secret Birthday Message, The Mixed-Up Chameleon, The Tiny Seed,* and *1,2,3 to the Zoo.*

RELATED CHILDREN'S BOOKS

May I Bring a Friend? by Beatrice Schenk deRegniers
Where Is My Friend? by Betsy Maestro and Giulio Maestro
Who Will Be My Friend? by Syd Hoff
Nettie Jo's Friends by Patricia C. McKissack
Frog and Toad Are Friends by Arnold Lobel

Project for *Do You Want to Be My Friend?*

DIRECTIONS

U.S. postage stamps have different kinds of illustrations on them. Presidents, flowers, birds, space discoveries, famous people, and shells have all been used.

You can pretend that you have been asked by the U.S. Postal Service to create a series of three new postage stamps, each of which should have a different illustration relating to *Do You Want to Be My Friend?* Work together to design and create new stamps (based on animals in the book) in the spaces below.

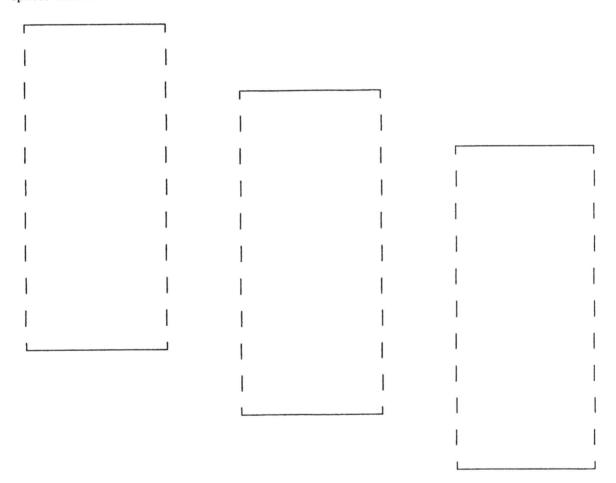

From *Involving Parents through Children's Literature: Grades 1-2,* 1992 • Libraries Unlimited, Inc. • P.O. Box 6633, Englewood, CO 80155-6633

Doctor DeSoto

William Steig
(New York: Scholastic, 1982)

STORY SUMMARY

This is a tale of wit versus might. Dr. and Mrs. DeSoto run the best dental clinic in town. Although the DeSotos are tiny mice, they work on patients as big as cows. One day Dr. DeSoto decides to help a big fox in pain. When the fox is about to give in to temptation, he finds he has been outfoxed.

DISCUSSION QUESTIONS

1. What strategy would you have used to outfox the fox if you had been in Dr. DeSoto's place?

2. How do you think the story would have ended if Mrs. DeSoto's plan had not worked?

3. What other animals do you think would be a threat to Dr. and Mrs. DeSoto?

4. Would you like for Dr. DeSoto to be your dentist? Why or why not?

ACTIVITIES (Please choose any two activities.)

1. As you read the story, stop when you reach the part where Mrs. DeSoto says, "I have a plan." Have your child predict what happens next and write down the prediction. Finish the story and talk about the prediction and the actual ending.

2. During a visit ask your dentist to talk with your child about proper dental care. Get some brochures, if available, and discuss them. Develop an original brochure on dental care for all children.

3. Discuss ways in which our diet would be different if we had no teeth. Make a list of foods that must be chewed and another list of foods that do not need to be chewed. Which list is longest?

4. Obtain some kitchen oven-fired clay or air-dry clay from a local hobby, variety, or art store. Work together to create an oversized model of a tooth. Be sure to display this tooth for the family to enjoy.

5. You may enjoy reading other books by William Steig, including *The Amazing Bone, Sylvester and the Magic Pebble*, and *The Real Thief*.

RELATED CHILDREN'S BOOKS

Fox Eyes by Margaret Wise
Rosie's Walk by Pat Hutchins
Bear's Toothache by David McPhail
Arthur's Tooth by Marc Brown

Frog and Toad Are Friends
Arnold Lobel
(New York: Harper & Row, 1970)

STORY SUMMARY

This is a collection of five short stories about two friends—a frog and a toad. One story deals with the coming of spring, another tells about a special story, and a third is about a missing button. Two other stories concern a funny bathing suit and an important letter.

DISCUSSION QUESTIONS

1. Why do you think Frog and Toad are such good friends?

2. What does the word *friendship* mean to you?

3. What are some of the special things friends do for each other?

4. Which of the five stories did you enjoy most? Why?

5. If you could say anything to Frog and Toad, what would you like to say?

ACTIVITIES (Please choose any two activities.)

1. Create a Frog and Toad Museum. Together collect several "artifacts" mentioned in the stories (e.g., buttons, a letter, a bathing suit, etc.) and place them in a large flat box (like one from a nearby bakery). Label each artifact according to which story it is in. Cover the box with clear plastic wrap so it looks like a museum case.

2. Create a new adventure for Frog and Toad. Your child may dictate or write an original story to be shared with the family.

3. Write a letter to Toad. What would your child want to say? Make a mailbox from a milk carton or small box and paint it red and blue. Take the role of Toad and respond to your child's letter.

4. Make a list of all the different types of animals used as motifs for commercial products (tigers, bears, cats, etc.). How many different animals are there? Do any commercial products (cereals, cars, toys) use frogs or toads as symbols.

5. Your child will enjoy other books about Frog and Toad, including *Frog and Toad All Year, Days with Frog and Toad, Frog and Toad Together*, and *The Frog and Toad Pop-up Book*.

RELATED CHILDREN'S BOOKS

Alexander and the Wind-Up Mouse by Leo Lionni
George and Martha by James Marshall
The Friend by John Burningham
Duck Goes Fishing by Judy Delton
Petunia by Roger Duvoisin
Best Friends by Steven Kellogg
Frog on His Own by Mercer Mayer

Project for *Frog and Toad Are Friends*

DIRECTIONS

Pretend that you and your child are newspaper reporters assigned to do a story on Frog and Toad. However, because of a short deadline, you can interview only one character. Which one would you choose?

_____

Now make up a list with your child of eight questions to ask that character. Write them in the spaces below. Ask questions that will produce some interesting information to share with the newspaper readers.

1. _____

_____

2. _____

_____

3. _____

_____

4. _____

_____

5. _____

_____

6. _____

_____

7. _____

_____

8. _____

_____

Together you may wish to role-play the reporter and the specific character (Frog or Toad).

George and Martha
James Marshall
(Boston: Houghton Mifflin, 1972)

STORY SUMMARY

George and Martha seem to know full well the joys and delights of having a friend to cheer you and to care, someone who will tell you the truth and go to great lengths to spare your feelings.

DISCUSSION QUESTIONS

1. What could you do with a hippopotamus for a friend?

2. If you could give George advice, what would it be?

3. Do you think your friends would enjoy this book? Why?

4. What other kinds of adventures could George and Martha have?

5. What have you learned about friendship that you did not already know?

6. How could you be a friend to someone who does not have a friend?

ACTIVITIES (Please choose any two activities.)

1. Work with your child and draw the outline of a hippopotamus on a sheet of paper. Obtain some dried peas and glue them around the outline of the hippo. Be sure your child has a place to display the three-dimensional poster.

2. Check in a cookbook for a recipe for split pea soup. Prepare the recipe with your child and serve it to the family. Create an original name for the soup, such as "Hippo's Happy Split Pea Soup" or "Practically Perfect Pea Soup."

3. Have your child choose an animal to have as a best friend. Ask your child to write a short story about the friendship he or she shares with the selected animal. For example, what would they say to each other, what would they do for fun, and where would they go?

4. Your child may enjoy writing to a pen pal in another part of the country or another part of the world. Write to Student Letter Exchange (215 5th Avenue S.E., Wasecu, MN 56093) for information.

RELATED CHILDREN'S BOOKS

Always and Forever Friends by C. Adler
Teach Me about Friends by Joy Berry
Friends by Helen Oxenbury
A Very Special Friend by Dorothy Levi
George and Martha Rise and Shine by James Marshall
George and Martha Encore by James Marshall
Frog and Toad Together by Arnold Lobel
Winnie-the-Pooh by A. A. Milne
Charlotte's Web by E. B. White
George and Martha Round and Round by James Marshall
Where Is My Friend? by Syd Hoff

The Gingerbread Boy
Paul Galdone
(Boston: Houghton Mifflin, 1975)

STORY SUMMARY

An old lady bakes a delightful gingerbread boy; but he runs away. No one can catch him except for a very crafty fox who gets the last laugh, or rather, the last bite!

DISCUSSION QUESTIONS

1. Are there some people you should trust and other people you should not trust?

2. What do you think would have happened if the fox had not been able to outsmart the gingerbread boy?

3. Why do you think the author wrote this story?

4. If you were asked to write a new ending for the story, what would you change? Why?

5. Would you enjoy reading this book again?

ACTIVITIES (Please choose any two activities.)

1. Purchase a box of gingerbread mix. Work with your child to make some gingerbread cookies or gingerbread boys. Your child may enjoy re-creating the story using one of the gingerbread boys the two of you bake.

2. Have your child create a gingerbread boy from construction paper, buttons, glue, and glitter.

3. Have your child dictate or write a sequel to the story pretending that the gingerbread boy escapes from the fox.

4. Together make a tape recording of this story. You can alternate parts and record various sections of the book.

5. Invite your child to create a song about the gingerbread boy. Take a popular tune such as "Row, Row, Row Your Boat" or "She'll Be Comin' 'Round the Mountain" and write some new lyrics for the music. Sing the song for other family members.

6. Write the word *gingerbread* on a large sheet of paper. Work with your child to see how many smaller words you can create using the letters in *gingerbread*, for example, *bad, need, read, grab, ring.*

RELATED CHILDREN'S BOOKS BY PAUL GALDONE

The Little Red Hen	*The Monkey and the Crocodile*
The Three Billy Goats Gruff	*Henny Penny*
Three Aesop Fox Fables	*The Horse, the Fox, and the Lion*
The Three Little Pigs	*Little Tuppan*

Project for *The Gingerbread Boy*

DIRECTIONS

In the following chart the column on the left lists the similarities between gingerbread children and real children. The column on the rights lists the differences. Complete this chart with your child adding some of his or her own words to both columns.

SIMILARITIES	DIFFERENCES
two hands	
	eye color
two feet	
	shape of ears
one head	
	hair color
one nose	
	height

From *Involving Parents through Children's Literature: Grades 1-2*, 1992 • Libraries Unlimited, Inc. • P.O. Box 6633, Englewood, CO 80155-6633

Gregory, the Terrible Eater
Mitchell Sharmat
(New York: Four Winds, 1980)

STORY SUMMARY

Gregory, a goat, is very picky about what he eats. Although most goats like to eat leather shoes and cans, Gregory prefers to eat fruits and vegetables. Finally, a helpful doctor discovers a "cure."

DISCUSSION QUESTIONS

1. What are some of your favorite foods? What are some of your least favorite foods?

2. Do you eat everything your parents tell you to eat? Why do you think they always make you eat things you do not want to?

3. Do you think Gregory would have eventually grown out of his unusual eating habits? Why?

4. What would have happened if Gregory's parents had not worked the "goat food" into his diet? Are there any foods you are glad your parents made you try?

ACTIVITIES (Please choose any two activities.)

1. Ask your child to cut out several pictures from old magazines. The pictures should be foods your child enjoys and some your child does not enjoy. Paste these pictures on a sheet of construction paper in two sections: Foods I Like and Foods I Don't Like.

2. Ask your child to create some menus of their favorite meals at home. Work with your child to compile these into a booklet.

3. Have your child pretend that a goat is coming to dinner. Give your child a paper plate and a variety of craft materials to use for food. For example, have your child create a tinfoil hamburger, button beans, yarn spaghetti, etc.

4. Challenge your child to create a television commercial to "sell" his or her favorite food. Give your child an opportunity to produce the commercial for other family members.

5. Research the actual diet of a goat as well as the diets of other animals. Use *Animal Encyclopedia for Children* by Roger Few (New York: Macmillan, 1991) as a reference. You and your child can make a comparative chart for the diets of the animals.

6. You may enjoy the story *The 300 Pound Cat* by Rosamond Dauer (New York: Avon, 1981). Have your child compare the eating habits of William (in *The 300 Pound Cat*) to Gregory (in *Gregory, the Terrible Eater*). How are the stories similar? How are they different?

RELATED CHILDREN'S BOOKS

An Apple a Day by Judi Barrett
We'll Have a Friend for Lunch by Jane Flory
Sheldon's Lunch by Bruce Lemerise
Alexander's Midnight Snack by Catherine Stock
Alexandra the Rock-Eater by Dorothy Van Woerkon

Harry the Dirty Dog
Gene Zion
(New York: Harper & Row, 1956)

STORY SUMMARY

Harry, the family dog, runs away from home when he thinks he is going to get a bath. After a full day of all sorts of dirty activities, he returns home where nobody recognizes him.

DISCUSSION QUESTIONS

1. How do you feel when you have to take a bath? How do you feel when you have to do something you do not want to do?

2. What do you think was the funniest part of the story? Why?

3. If you had a dog like Harry, how would you get him to take a bath?

4. What kind of animal makes the best pet? Why?

5. What are some places you like to visit in your neighborhood? In how many of them would you get dirty?

6. What kinds of tricks would you like to teach Harry?

ACTIVITIES (Please choose any two activities.)

1. Together make a tape recording of this story. As you read the story into a recorder, have your child create some sound effects or background noises (dog barking, water running, train whistle, etc.). Play the taped version for other members of the family.

2. Work with your child to create an original book on the care of family pets. Encourage your child to record specific tips for people on taking care of a pet. Your local veterinarian or pet store will have some brochures or information your child will find helpful for his or her original guide.

3. Purchase several different kinds of soap. Allow your child to examine the soaps and describe their similarities and differences. Record this information on a large sheet of newsprint.

4. Have your child look in the yellow pages of the local phone book and compile a list of all the services related to dogs (veterinarians, pet stores, guide dogs, grooming services, etc.).

RELATED CHILDREN'S BOOKS

Digby and Kate by Barbara Baker
Singing Sam by Clyde R. Bulla
Ginger Jumps by Lisa Campbell Ernst
Barkley by Syd Hoff
I Want a Dog by Dayal Kaur Khalsa
Lily Takes a Walk by Satoshi Kitamura

Project for *Harry the Dirty Dog*

DIRECTIONS

Work with your child to write an imaginary letter to Harry telling him why he should come home. Be sure to emphasize some of the benefits of home life as opposed to life on the streets.

_____ (date)

Mr. Harry Dog
123 Main Street
Anyplace, PA 12345

Dear Harry:

_____

_____

_____

_____

_____

_____

_____

_____

_____

_____

_____

Sincerely,

_____

(signature)

From *Involving Parents through Children's Literature: Grades 1-2*, 1992 • Libraries Unlimited, Inc. • P.O. Box 6633, Englewood, CO 80155-6633

Ira Sleeps Over

Bernard Waber
(Boston: Houghton Mifflin, 1972)

STORY SUMMARY

Ira is invited to sleep over at his friend's house. However, he has one small problem: should he bring his teddy bear along? But Ira discovers that he is not the only one with a teddy bear.

DISCUSSION QUESTIONS

1. How would the story have been different if Reggie had not had a teddy bear?

2. Where do you think Reggie and Ira got the names for their teddy bears?

3. Why do you think Ira's sister made so much fun of him?

4. If you spent the night at a friend's house, what would you want to do for fun?

ACTIVITIES (Please choose any two activities.)

1. Have your child create bear collages by cutting out pictures of various bears from old magazines. Have your child paste them onto large pieces of paper.

2. Have your child create a written or oral story from the perspective of Tah-Tah. Does your child think that Tah-Tah might have felt neglected?

3. Have your child pretend that he or she is a news reporter for a local television station. Make up a series of questions he or she would like to ask Ira. You can take on the role of Ira and respond to the questions your child asks.

4. Talk with your child about some of his or her bedtime routines (watch TV, take a bath, put pajamas on, say goodnight to parents, etc.). Make up a list and post it in your child's room.

5. Have your child write an invitation to Ira to sleep at his or her house. Be sure to include all of the activities planned.

6. Together make some stamps out of vegetables. For example, cut a potato in half and scratch a design on the cut part with a fork. Have your child press the potato stamp on an inked stamp pad and transfer the design to a sheet of paper. Experiment with different designs. Try using other vegetables or fruits for the stamps.

7. Have your child create a pajama catalog. Search through old catalogs and magazines for pictures of pajamas. Cut out several examples and paste them on sheets of construction paper. Staple the sheets together to create an original catalog.

RELATED CHILDREN'S BOOKS

A Bear Called Paddington by Michael Bond
Bears in Pairs by Niki Yektai
Not This Bear! by Bernice Myers
Jake and Rosie by Patricia Lillie
Jamaica's Find by Juanita Havill

Project for *Ira Sleeps Over*

DIRECTIONS

Work with your child to list six features of teddy bears in the left-hand column. In the right-hand column list six features of real bears. Draw lines connecting those characteristics shared by teddy bears and real bears.

<table>
<tr><td>**TEDDY BEARS**</td><td>**REAL BEARS**</td></tr>
<tr><td>_____</td><td>_____</td></tr>
<tr><td>_____</td><td>_____</td></tr>
<tr><td>_____</td><td>_____</td></tr>
<tr><td>_____</td><td>_____</td></tr>
<tr><td>_____</td><td>_____</td></tr>
<tr><td>_____</td><td>_____</td></tr>
</table>

Leo the Late Bloomer

Robert Kraus
(New York: Windmill Books, 1971)

STORY SUMMARY

Leo the tiger takes his time growing up. His parents are patient, and he eventually begins to bloom.

DISCUSSION QUESTIONS

1. What makes Leo such an interesting character?

2. How would you feel if you were a late bloomer?

3. What does the term *late bloomer* mean to you?

4. If you were Leo's friend, how would you treat him?

5. What part of the book would you change if you could? Why?

ACTIVITIES (Please choose any two activities.)

1. Obtain a large sheet of newsprint at an art or hobby store. Have your child lie down on the paper while you trace his or her outline. Have your child cut out the outline and write randomly within the outline (or dictate for you to write) words that best describe him or her. Hang the outline in your child's room. Encourage your child to think of other words to be added to the outline periodically.

2. Together make casts of your child's feet or hands. Use the following recipe for flour dough:

   > 2 cups self-rising flour
   > 2 tablespoons alum (available at large drug stores)
   > 2 tablespoons salt
   > 2 tablespoons cooking oil
   > 1 cup + 2 tablespoons boiling water

   Carefully mix all ingredients and knead until a doughy consistency. Roll out some of the mixture and have your child press a hand or foot into the mixture. Put the cast outside in the sun or bake in an oven (250°) for several hours. The casts can be painted and kept for several months. Your child may wish to make additional ones to compare his or her growth during that period.

3. Have your child plant a bean or radish seed in a paper cup filled with potting soil. Talk about how, even though you cannot see the seed growing inside the soil, it will germinate and grow. Your child can observe the cup every other day and keep a journal on the growth of the seed. Compare the hidden growth of the seed to the hidden growth of Leo.

RELATED CHILDREN'S BOOKS

You Are Much Too Small by Betty Boegehold
Growing Up by Kevin Henkes
My Very First Book of Growth by Eric Carle

The Growing Story by Ruth Krauss
All by Myself by Anna Grossnickle Hines
Next Year I'll Be Special by Patricia Reilly Giff

Little Bear
Else Homelund Minarik
(New York: Harper & Row, 1957)

STORY SUMMARY

This is the story of Little Bear and four of his adventures. In the first chapter, he goes outside to play in the snow but gets cold and asks his mother for something to wear. In the second chapter, he cannot find his birthday cake, so he makes birthday soup. He experiences an imaginary trip to the moon in the third chapter; and in the fourth chapter, Little Bear and his mother remember all his adventures.

DISCUSSION QUESTIONS

1. How would you travel to the moon?

2. What would you do if you did not have a birthday cake?

3. Why did Little Bear's friends choose honey, a wildflower, and an apple for his birthday presents?

4. What would you bring Little Bear for his birthday?

5. What makes Little Bear such a lovable character?

6. Would your friends enjoy reading this book? Why?

ACTIVITIES (Please choose any two activities.)

1. Together make a snow shaker. Obtain a small baby food jar. Using the lid of the jar as a base, glue a small plastic figure or animal on the inside of the lid with waterproof household cement. Put a small amount of white glitter in the jar and fill with water. Put a line of glue around the inside of the lid where it comes in contact with the jar. Glue the lid to the jar and allow it to dry thoroughly before inverting.

2. Have your child paint murals depicting outside scenes from each of the four seasons. Frame each scene with pieces of cardboard, and display them in his or her bedroom or the living room.

3. Your child may enjoy pantomiming snow activities such as having a snowball fight, making snow angels, riding on a sled, building a snowman, etc. This can be a free-form rhythmic activity by performing the motions to music, such as Beethoven's *Menuett-Minuet* (available as a cassette tape from Delta Music, Inc., Los Angeles, CA [catalog No. MC79-819]).

4. Work with your child to make a four-season mobile. Use the straight wire from the bottom of two coat hangers. Cut two wires of equal length and fasten them together in the shape of a cross. Tie them securely in the center. Leave one of the tying strings long enough to use as a hanger. Ask your child to draw and color items that remind him or her of each of the four seasons; for example, a swimsuit, a boot, a snowflake, a beach ball, a flower, a sun, a colored leaf, etc. Tie all of the items from one season to one of the four ends of the mobile and do likewise for the other three seasons. Hang the mobile in your child's room.

5. Have your child plan and hold a birthday party for his or her stuffed animals.

   a. Make invitations in the shape of the animals using cardboard and crayons. The invitations can be addressed to "Dear Friend" or "Dear Relative."

   b. Together decide on the food to serve. Make menus based on the format of the menu from a local restaurant.

   c. For a centerpiece, make a giant birthday cake out of cardboard, using a hat box or other box painted in birthday colors.

   d. Make bear-shaped cookies. Use any recipe that requires the cookie dough to be rolled out. Instead of using a cookie cutter, use a knife to cut the dough into bear shapes.

   Decorate with canned frosting, candy stick-ons, colored sugar, and chocolate jimmies.

6. Direct your child to write a letter to a relative or other special person telling about the best surprise he or she ever had.

7. Take your child bird watching in the wild or at the zoo. Talk about how birds fly. Have your child make a seed and bean mosaic of the bird he or she likes best. Use oak tagboard or cardboard for the base. Provide various seeds, rice, beans, and macaroni in many different colors. Draw an outline of a bird on the cardboard. Glue the seeds and beans to the cardboard in the shape of the bird. Allow to dry and hang in the family room.

8. Direct your child to make a tabletop model of a castle using sugar cubes glued together with icing. Decorate with lifesavers, cake decorations, cinnamon candies, etc.

9. Have your child tell about what he or she would bring as a gift for Little Bear if invited to his party.

10. Ask your child to dictate or write a sequel to the book, describing some of the things Little Bear will do when he is older; the story could be called, for example, "Teen Bear."

RELATED CHILDREN'S BOOKS

Paddington at the Zoo by Michael Bond
Bear and Duck on the Run by Judy Delton
Bertie and the Bear by Pamela Allen
Jesse Bear, What Will You Wear? by Nancy Carlstrom

The Little House
Virginia Lee Burton
(Boston: Houghton Mifflin, 1942)

STORY SUMMARY

A beautiful house is built in the country. The little house loves the country but is curious about life in the city. As time passes, a city grows up around the little house and the little house finds that city life is not for her.

DISCUSSION QUESTIONS

1. How do you think the little house felt about the city growing up around her?

2. Would you want to live in the little house? Why or why not?

3. What would be the best kind of house to live in?

4. What season of the year do you enjoy the most? If you had been the little house, which season would you have enjoyed the most?

ACTIVITIES (Please choose any two activities.)

1. Have your child pretend he or she is the little house. Ask your child to write a thank-you letter to the great-great-granddaughter for moving the little house back to the country.

2. Discuss some of the advantages of living in the city. What are some advantages of living in the country? If your child had a choice, where would he or she prefer to live? Would it make any difference if your child was, instead of a person, an inanimate object like a house?

3. Read the story of Hansel and Gretel to your child. Talk about real and make-believe houses. Invite your child to create a story about a house of some other edible material, such as spaghetti or swiss cheese. Allow your child to draw illustrations of his or her edible house.

4. Have your child make an identification card for the little house (similar to a driver's license). What information should be included on the I.D. card besides the address?

5. Provide your child with several boxes of various sizes (shoe boxes, cardboard boxes, milk cartons). Paint the boxes various colors using tempera paints (available at any art or hobby store). Create a miniature city using the boxes as houses and other buildings.

6. Take a walk with your child through your neighborhood. If possible, take photographs of various houses. When the pictures are developed, have your child arrange them into a scrapbook and label them. Be sure to talk about the differences and similarities among houses.

RELATED CHILDREN'S BOOKS

The Wonderful House by Margaret Wise Brown
Best Little House by Aileen Fisher
A House Is a House for Me by Mary Ann Hoberman
A Very Special House by Ruth Krauss
I Can Build a House by Shigeo Watanabe

Project for *The Little House*

DIRECTIONS

Work together to write a letter to your house telling it what you like most about living there.

Dear House:

Sincerely,

Make Way for Ducklings
Robert McCloskey
(New York: Viking Press, 1969)

STORY SUMMARY

Mr. and Mrs. Mallard Duck look for just the right place to raise their ducklings. After searching the country and city, they decide to settle on a nice quiet island.

DISCUSSION QUESTIONS

1. Where would you choose as a safe place for a duck family?

2. Why would the woods be a dangerous place to raise ducklings?

3. If you were a police officer, how would you help the ducks?

4. How would this story be different if the main characters were pigs instead of ducks?

ACTIVITIES (Please choose any two activities.)

1. Encourage your child to make a poster consisting of a list of rules for raising ducks. What procedures would people have to follow to ensure the safety of ducks?

2. Have your child create puppets by drawing illustrations of selected characters from the story on cardboard, cutting out the figures, and gluing them to Popsicle™ sticks. Provide your child with an opportunity to present a small theatrical production using several of the puppets.

3. Invite your child to select one of the eight ducklings and write a biography about the duckling after it is fully grown (e.g., where the duckling decides to move, if it gets married, etc.).

4. Help your child locate Boston on a map of the United States or world. Ask your child to think of reasons why the mallards may have been flying over Boston. Talk about why ducks fly south in the fall and north in the spring.

5. Work with your child to carve figures of several ducks from soap (use a table knife and Ivory™ soap). Float these in the bathtub and retell the story while your child takes a bath.

6. Ask your child what he or she would have named the eight ducklings. Send out imaginary birth announcements for the ducklings.

7. Talk with your child about safety precautions to take when crossing the street. Work together to design a safety mural of important street-crossing procedures.

RELATED CHILDREN'S BOOKS

Happy Birthday, Dear Duck by Eve Bunting
The Duck with Squeaky Feet by Denys Cazet
Q Is for Duck by Mary Elting
Duckling Sees by Hargrave Hands
Quack? by Mischa Richter

Mike Mulligan and His Steam Shovel
Virginia Lee Burton
(Boston: Houghton Mifflin, 1939)

STORY SUMMARY

This is the story of the relationship between a construction worker and his faithful steam shovel. Competition from gas- and diesel-powered shovels was a constant challenge. Mike and Mary Anne dig the foundation for the Popperville town hall in record time. Mary Anne is remodeled as a furnace and Mike becomes the town hall janitor.

DISCUSSION QUESTIONS

1. What would you have suggested for getting Mary Anne out of the hole?

2. How would you describe the people of Popperville?

3. Do you believe Mary Anne could really dig in a day as much as 100 men in a week? Why?

4. Why do you think Mike named his shovel Mary Anne?

5. Would Mary Anne make a good shovel today? Why? Why not?

ACTIVITIES (Please choose any two activities.)

1. Have your child pretend to be a news reporter and conduct a make-believe news broadcast from Popperville during the digging of the hole. You can take on the role of one of the townspeople for your child to interview.

2. Invite your child to dictate or rewrite the story from Mary Anne's point of view.

3. Take your child to the local public library and ask the librarian for books on the history of railroads or machines. Share these books with your child and talk about how railroads and machines have changed over the years.

4. Talk with your child about the differences and similarities between cities and rural areas. Ask your child to prepare a list to post in his or her room.

5. Reread the story to your child and during the retelling ask him or her to pantomime the actions of Mary Anne.

6. Ask your child to make up a conversation between the new town hall of Popperville and a very large skyscraper from New York. What would the two ask each other or talk about?

RELATED CHILDREN'S BOOKS

Night in the Country by Cynthia Rylant
Heavy Equipment by Jan Adkins
Dig, Drill, Dump, Fill by Watty Piper
Town and Country by Alice Provensen
Mountains by Michael Johnstone
Motor Trucks by Russell Hoban

Project for *Mike Mulligan and His Steam Shovel*

DIRECTIONS

Work together to list in the second column of this sheet some of the things your child does on a typical Saturday. Then list the activities Mike Mulligan and Mary Anne might do on a typical Saturday. Remember, there are no right or wrong answers.

	YOUR CHILD	MIKE MULLIGAN	MARY ANNE
7:00			
8:30			
10:00			
11:30			
1:00			
2:30			
4:00			
5:30			
7:00			
8:30			
10:00			

Millions of Cats

Wanda Gag
(New York: Coward-McCann, 1956)

STORY SUMMARY

An old man and woman always wanted a cat. The old man set out to find one. As luck would have it, he finds a whole bunch of cats and brings them all home. The cats eventually solve the problem of too many cats, and the couple is finally left with one kitten.

DISCUSSION QUESTIONS

1. What would you do with a million cats?

2. What do you think the little kitten was thinking about when all the other cats were fighting?

3. Why do you think the cats followed the old man home?

4. How did the old lady feel when her husband brought all the cats home?

ACTIVITIES (Please choose any two activities.)

1. Ask your child to cut out pictures of several cats from some old magazines. Paste each picture on a separate piece of paper. Have your child dictate or write what he or she likes and dislikes most about each cat.

2. Work with your child to compile a list of facts about cats. List each fact on a separate index card and have your child list additional facts over a period of several weeks.

3. Take your child to the local animal shelter or SPCA. Take photographs of some of the cats there, and when the photos are developed have your child put together a scrapbook of cats. Your child can dictate or write some information about each cat for the scrapbook (e.g., name of each cat, where it lived, personality traits, etc.).

4. Have your child pretend that he or she is the last remaining kitten. Ask your child to write a thank-you letter to the old man and lady for the care they provided.

5. Work with your child and look for examples of cats in comic strips (e.g., Garfield, Heathcliff, Sylvester). Have your child create his or her own comic strip using an original cat.

6. Work with your child to list on one side of a sheet of paper the things he or she enjoys doing alone. On the other side of the paper, have your child list the things he or she enjoys doing with other people. Talk about the differences between the two lists.

RELATED CHILDREN'S BOOKS

Hi, Cat! by Ezra Jack Keats
Where Does My Cat Sleep? by Norma Simon
Cat on the Mat by Brian Wildsmith
Cat in the Hat by Dr. Seuss
Koko's Kitten by Francine Patterson

Project for *Millions of Cats*

DIRECTIONS

Have your child pretend that he or she is one of the cats in the book. Ask your child to draw pictures that answer each of the questions below.

What do you look like?   **Where do you live?**

What do you eat?   **Where do you sleep?**

Miss Nelson Is Missing!

Harry Allard
(Boston: Houghton Mifflin, 1977)

STORY SUMMARY

The students of Room 207 are the worst-behaved students of the school. Miss Nelson, their teacher, suddenly disappears and Miss Viola Swamp arrives with hours of homework. The class tries to figure out what has happened to Miss Nelson.

DISCUSSION QUESTIONS

1. When you had a substitute, how was she similar to Miss Swamp? How was your substitute different?

2. Would you want to have Miss Nelson as a teacher?

3. How do you feel about having a substitute teacher like Viola Swamp?

4. If you were Detective McSmogg, where would you have started looking for Miss Nelson? Why?

5. How would you have felt if you had been one of the students when Miss Nelson returned? Why?

ACTIVITIES (Please choose any two activities.)

1. Have your child make a "Wanted" poster for Miss Nelson. What kind of information should be included on the poster? Post the finished poster on the door of the refrigerator.

2. Talk with your child about some of the qualities of a good teacher. What should good teachers do? How should they act toward their students?

3. Ask your child to dictate or write a sequel to the story. Have Detective McSmogg looking for Miss Viola Swamp. Where would he look for her? Would he ever find her?

4. There are two sequels to this story, *Miss Nelson Is Back* and *Miss Nelson Has a Field Day*.

5. Ask your child to look through several old magazines and cut out pictures of children he or she would like to have as classmates. Paste these pictures on a large sheet of paper. Talk about why these children would make up an ideal class.

6. Have your child write a letter to Miss Nelson asking her to come back to the classroom. What would your child say to convince Miss Nelson that she should return?

RELATED CHILDREN'S BOOKS

Encyclopedia Brown by Donald Sobol (series)
The Case of the Cat's Meow by Crosby Bonsall
The Homework Caper by Joan Lexaw
Something Queer Is Going On by Elizabeth Levy

The Mitten

Alvin Tresselt
(New York: Scholastic, 1964)

STORY SUMMARY

A little boy is out in the woods gathering wood for his grandmother. On his trip, he loses a mitten. The story tells what becomes of the mitten when animals in the forest decide to crawl inside to keep warm.

DISCUSSION QUESTIONS

1. How would the story be different if the boy had lost two mittens?

2. How would the story change if the bear had been the first animal inside the mitten?

3. Would the story have changed if the boy had been walking through a city?

4. What animal in the story would you like to be? Why?

ACTIVITIES (Please choose any two activities.)

1. Work with your child to create a vest like the one the bear wore. Cut out a head hole and two armholes from a grocery bag. Decorate the bag to resemble the vest the bear wore. Retell the story with your child wearing his or her vest.

2. Provide your child with a piece of blue construction paper, a bag of white cotton balls, and glue, so that he or she can create a snowy picture. Draw in trees, animals, and an illustration of the boy.

3. Provide your child with several old magazines, catalogs, and calendars to cut out pictures depicting the four seasons. Glue one picture on each of four large index cards and arrange the cards in order. Post them on the refrigerator.

4. Cut out snowflakes from construction paper. To make a snowflake, have your child cut out a large circle. Fold the circle in half, and fold again. With a pair of scissors cut designs on both sides of the pie-shaped piece. Unfold the paper to see the beautiful snowflake. When the snowflake is completed, together retell the story from the snowflake's point of view.

5. Obtain an old sheet or blanket and pretend that the sheet or blanket is a giant mitten. Have your child pretend to be one of the animals as you retell the story.

6. Take your child to a park or nearby woods to look for animal tracks. Get a copy of *Secrets of a Wildlife Watcher* by Jim Arnosky (New York: Lothrop, Lee, & Shepard Books, 1983) as a resource.

RELATED CHILDREN'S BOOKS

The First Snowfall by Anne and Harlow Rockwell
The Snowy Day by Ezra Jack Keats
First Snow by Emily Arnold McCully
Snow Lion by David McPhail

No Roses for Harry

Gene Zion
(New York: Harper & Row, 1958)

STORY SUMMARY

Harry, the family dog, receives a sweater from his grandmother for his birthday. Harry does not like the sweater and does everything he can think of to get rid of it. Finally, the sweater becomes a bird's nest. Harry's grandmother makes him a sweater he likes.

DISCUSSION QUESTIONS

1. Do you think you would like to have Harry as a pet? Why or why not?

2. If you were Harry, where would you have tried to lose the sweater?

3. Why do you think Harry disliked the sweater with the roses on it?

4. If you were the author of the book, would you have changed the ending?

ACTIVITIES (Please choose any two activities.)

1. Have your child make an original birthday card for Harry. Fold a piece of thin cardboard in half to form a greeting card. Have your child illustrate the cover and write a greeting on the inside.

2. Visit a local pet store to see the different kinds of dogs. Talk with your child about the varieties available. Ask your child about the qualities necessary for a dog to become a good pet. Why does your child prefer one type of dog over another?

3. Ask your child to write a thank-you letter from Harry to Grandmother concerning a new sweater. What should be written? Should any mention be made of the original sweater?

4. Create a bird garland. You need a blunt needle, heavy-duty thread, raisins, stale bread, popcorn, and cheese bits. String the edible ingredients onto the thread. Hang the bird garland in a nearby tree. Ask your child to observe the variety of birds that eat from the garland.

5. Your child may enjoy other books about Harry, including *Harry and the Lady Next Door* and *Harry by the Sea*.

RELATED CHILDREN'S BOOKS

My Dog and the Birthday Mystery by David Adler
The First Dog by Jan Breet
Dog for a Day by Marjorie Flack
Benji and the Barking Dog by Margret Bloy Graham
Scruffy by Jack Stonely
Old Mother Hubbard and Her Dog by Lennart Hellsing
A Dog's Life by Lee Bennett Hopkins
A Puppy Who Wanted a Boy by Jane Thayer
Alfred by Janice May Udry
Dogs and Puppies by Rose Hill

Nothing Ever Happens on My Block
Ellen Raskin
(New York: Atheneum, 1966)

STORY SUMMARY

Chester Folbert does not think anything ever happens on his block. But, if he took notice, he would see that there are a number of exciting things going on right in front of his eyes.

DISCUSSION QUESTIONS

1. What would you do if you found a lot of money?

2. What kinds of things happen on your street? On your block?

3. What do you like to do when you are bored?

4. What is the most exciting thing that has ever happened to you on your block?

5. What is the most exciting thing that has happened to you in your house?

ACTIVITIES (Please choose any two activities.)

1. Have your child create a book about his or her neighborhood. Have your child illustrate some important buildings, streets, and trees and flowers near your home. Ask your child to dictate or write about some of the important sites.

2. Show your child a copy of the town newspaper. Ask your child to create an imaginary newspaper for your neighborhood. What sports events take place there? What would be some front-page headlines? What about the weather?

3. Have your child draw a picture of the most exciting thing that has ever happened in the neighborhood. Post it on the door of the refrigerator along with a blank sheet of paper. Have other family members write down their memories of that event. Discuss any differences between what the child remembers and what other family members remember about the event.

4. Take a walking tour of your community. Provide your child with a camera to take photos or draw pictures of buildings, houses, and other important landmarks. Talk about what makes your neighborhood or community special.

5. Work with your child to make a calendar of home events. Record special family events or upcoming television programs in the boxes of a wall calendar. Refer to the calendar frequently and record additional events.

RELATED CHILDREN'S BOOKS

Once around the Block by Kevin Henkes
Our Village by John Yeoman
We Never Get to Do Anything by Martha G. Alexander
Nothing to Do by Russell Hoban
Bored—Nothing to Do! by Peter Spier

Project for *Nothing Ever Happens on My Block*

DIRECTIONS

To write a name poem take a name (such as a person's name or the name of a city) and write it vertically on a sheet of paper. Then, make each letter in the name stand for a word or phrase that describes the person or city. Here is a name poem for New York:

Near the ocean

East of Chicago

Wonderful entertainment

Yonkers (a borough)

Old people and young people

Really large

King Kong

Have your child name your neighborhood, community, town, or city. Write that name vertically in the space below. Ask your child to suggest a descriptive word or phrase for each letter. Be sure to talk about why your child chooses particular words.

Pancakes for Breakfast

Tomie dePaola
(New York: Harcourt Brace Jovanovich, 1978)

STORY SUMMARY

This is the story of a woman who wants pancakes for breakfast. A series of events eventually leads her to have pancakes at her neighbor's house.

DISCUSSION QUESTIONS

1. What is your favorite breakfast food?

2. Which do you enjoy more—homemade pancakes or pancakes served in a restaurant? Why?

3. How would you feel if you came home and found that your pets had destroyed your kitchen?

4. At the end of the story there is a picture frame containing the following saying: "If at first you do not succeed, try, try again." What does that mean?

5. What is your favorite breakfast food? What is your favorite lunch food? What is your favorite dinner food? Could you live on just those three foods for a whole year? Why? Why not?

ACTIVITIES (Please choose any two activities.)

1. Have your child cut out several round shapes from sheets of paper. Decorate each one as though it were a pancake. On the back of each one have your child paste pictures cut from old magazines of different pancake ingredients (flour, milk, shortening, etc.). Be sure the "pancakes" are displayed for all to enjoy.

2. Have your child create an imaginary story on the life of a pancake. How did that pancake come to be? What did it do during its life? And how did it finally end up? Your child may wish to dictate or write a story pretending that he or she is the pancake.

3. Look through several cookbooks. Select a variety of pancake recipes to share with your child, and choose one to create together. Later, prepare other versions.

4. Take your child on a field trip to a local restaurant. Obtain prices for different breakfast foods and, if possible, collect the menu. Talk about the variety of foods served in a restaurant and the different prices charged.

5. Your child will enjoy reading other books by Tomie dePaola, including *Charlie Needs a Cloak, The Legend of the Bluebonnet, When Everyone Was Fast Asleep*, and *Oliver Button Is a Sissy*.

RELATED CHILDREN'S BOOKS

Babar Learns to Cook by Laurent de Brunhoff
Teddybears Cookbook by Susanna Gretz
The Popcorn Book by Tomie dePaola
The Best of Friends by Josephine Aldridge
A Friend Is Someone Who Likes You by Joan Walsh Anglund

Project for *Pancakes for Breakfast*

DIRECTIONS

Work together to prepare a menu for an upcoming day. Have your child suggest food that can be served at breakfast, lunch, and dinner for the family. Make up the list now and have your child help you prepare and serve all the items at all three meals on the selected day.

DATE: _____

BREAKFAST	LUNCH	DINNER
_____	_____	_____
_____	_____	_____
_____	_____	_____
_____	_____	_____
_____	_____	_____
_____	_____	_____
_____	_____	_____

The Polar Express
Chris Van Allsburg
(Boston: Houghton Mifflin, 1985)

STORY SUMMARY

Late one Christmas Eve, a young boy is invited to board the Polar Express. The mysterious train takes the boy to the North Pole to meet Santa Claus, where he receives a special present.

DISCUSSION QUESTIONS

1. Why didn't the boy's mother and father hear the bell?

2. How do the illustrations in the book make you feel? How are these illustrations different from the illustrations in other books you have read?

3. Why do you think the bell still rings for the boy, even though he is older?

4. Why did the boy lose the bell?

5. Is this a good book to share at Christmas? Can this book be read at other times during the year?

6. Why do you think the author wrote this book? What would you like to say to the author?

ACTIVITIES (Please choose any two activities.)

1. Your child may enjoy making a whipped-cream picture. Spread some canned whipped cream or topping on a clean tabletop or large sheet of paper. Have your child use his or her fingers to copy one of the illustrations from the book into the whipped cream. The whipped cream represents snow and your child may eat some of the picture as it is being created.

2. In a letter to the author of the book, Chris Van Allsburg, allow your child to express his or her opinion of the book. The letters can be sent to: Chris Van Allsburg, c/o Houghton Mifflin Company, 2 Park Street, Boston, MA 02108. Make sure your child understands that he or she may not receive a reply due to the author's heavy writing and travel schedule.

3. Help your child create his or her own Polar Express milk carton train. You need empty milk cartons, tempera paints, liquid soap, brushes, scissors, and pipe cleaners. Mix the dry tempera paint and liquid soap (the soap makes the paint stick to the waxy surface of the milk carton). Have your child paint the cartons various colors. Cut the tops off the cartons, leaving a square open box. Holding the open side up, punch a hole in the front and back of the carton and insert a pipe cleaner on each side. On the inside of the carton tie each end of the pipe cleaners into large knots. Retell the story with your child manipulating his or her Polar Express.

4. Ask your child to dictate or write an imaginary story about what he or she would have done if asked to board the Polar Express.

5. Work with your child to create a fictitious newspaper about the Polar Express. You and your child can each submit advertisements, a comic strip, a schedule of trips, weather and travel advisories, etc. Put these all together in the form of a newspaper.

6. Ask your child to create a collage of transportation using pictures cut from magazines. Encourage your child to select various forms of transportation (e.g., cars, trains, trucks, airplanes, ships, bicycles, motorcycles, etc.) for the collage. Glue the selected pictures on a large sheet of construction paper and display it somewhere in the house.

7. Talk with your child about the importance of traffic signs and signals. Work together to make a list of common signs (STOP, Yield, No Left Turn, etc.). How are the signs similar? How are they different? Why are pictures or symbols used in place of words?

RELATED CHILDREN'S BOOKS

The Christmas Party by Adrienne Adams
Arthur's Christmas by Marc Brown
A Christmas Promise by Clark Carrier
Christmas Moon by Denys Cazet
Joy to Christmas by Beatrice Chute
The Christmas Box by Eve Merriam
Christmas Eve by Susie Stevenson
Nicky's Christmas Surprise by Harriet Ziefert
Snow before Christmas by Tasha Tudor

Rosie's Walk
Pat Hutchins
(New York: Macmillan, 1968)

STORY SUMMARY

Rosie the hen goes for a walk through the farm. She does not know there is a sly fox following her who just happens to get into all kinds of trouble.

DISCUSSION QUESTIONS

1. Do you think Rosie knew that the fox was following her? Why or why not?

2. Do you think the fox will come back?

3. What are some other places on a farm that Rosie could have walked to?

4. What do you think Rosie had for dinner?

5. Why do you think the fox was following Rosie?

ACTIVITIES (Please choose any two activities.)

1. Ask your child to suggest further actions for Rosie and to draw additional illustrations for the new actions.

2. Take a walk with your child around your neighborhood. Stop occasionally to allow your child to draw some illustrations of several sites. Upon your arrival home have your child staple the drawings together to create a personal "walk" book.

3. Ask your child to select one of the animals pictured in the book that was not mentioned in the reading and to dictate or write what that animal was thinking when Rosie and the fox walked past.

4. Read the book again, but this time ask your child to make the sounds of the animals as Rosie walks past them. Ask other family members to join in making animal sounds, too.

5. Have your child select three illustrations from the book. Talk with your child about what the fox is thinking after each disaster he encounters.

6. Ask your child to draw one or more illustrations of Rosie taking a walk in your backyard. What would she see? What other animals would she encounter?

RELATED CHILDREN'S BOOKS

Walk When the Moon Is Full by Frances Hamer
A Walk by the Pond by Wallace Kirkland
A Walk in the Snow by Phyllis S. Busch
Walk with Your Eyes by Marcia Brown

Project for *Rosie's Walk*

DIRECTIONS

Have your child pretend that he or she is going to start a brand-new farm in another state. What will the new farm need in the way of tools, buildings, animals, etc.? In each of the boxes below have your child draw illustrations of the items needed. Next to each picture put the quantity of that item needed to begin the farm.

What animals will you need?	What tools will you need?

Page 1 of a 2-page handout.

From *Involving Parents through Children's Literature: Grades 1-2*, 1992 • Libraries Unlimited, Inc. • P.O. Box 6633, Englewood, CO 80155-6633

What crops will you grow?	What buildings will you build?

The Snowy Day

Ezra Jack Keats
(New York: Viking Press, 1962)

STORY SUMMARY

Peter looks out his bedroom window one morning and sees snow all around. He spends a fun-filled day in the snow and comes home tired and wet. He is eager to play in the snow again the next day.

DISCUSSION QUESTIONS

1. How did Peter feel when he saw all the snow outside his window? Would you have felt the same way?

2. Why do you think Peter decided not to join the big boys in a snowball fight?

3. How would your life be different if it snowed year-round?

4. How do you think Peter felt when he discovered that his snowball had melted?

5. Do you like snow? Why or why not?

6. How might Peter's day have been different if it had rained instead of snowed?

ACTIVITIES (Please choose any two activities.)

1. Talk with your child about ways to keep warm during the winter. Check out books from your local public library on winter fashions for various parts of the country or around the world. You may wish to use the book *How to Keep Warm in Winter* by David A. Ross (New York: Crowell, 1980) as a reference.

2. Read your child the poem "First Snow," by Marie Louise Allen, in the *Random House Book of Poetry for Children* (New York: Random House, 1983). Talk about ways that snow can change the way everyday objects look. Discuss with your child new ways to think about snow. For example, snow may look like "icing on a house," or "lots of cotton balls on a fencepost." It may be helpful to have some pictures available for your child to look at for ideas.

3. Talk with your child about the role of Peter's mother in the story. How did she feel when Peter was playing in the snow? What was she doing while he was outside? How did she feel when he came back in with wet clothes? How did she feel about the snow? Invite your child to dictate or rewrite the story from the mother's point of view.

4. Work with your child to generate a list of winter sports. How many different winter sports can you and your child come up with? (Hint: think of some Winter Olympics sports.) Post the list and add to it when you can.

5. You and your child may enjoy learning about the formation of snow. Use *Snow and Ice* by Stephen Krensky (New York: Scholastic, 1989) as a reference.

6. Go through the book, and have your child identify the senses that Peter is using during each segment of his adventure in the snow. Generate a list of words that can be used to describe snow. Your child can write poems about the snow, describing it with the five senses. How does it look, feel, taste, smell, and sound?

7. Have your child write a sequel to *The Snowy Day*, describing Peter's adventures with his friend on the second day of snow. Have your child create pictures to illustrate the text by using paper cutouts, similar in style to the illustrations of Ezra Jack Keats.

8. Your child may enjoy learning about a special snow activity in Alaska. Call 1-800-545-MUSH, for a packet of information about the Iditarod Sled Dog Race, which begins the first Saturday of every March. The packet costs $2.00 and includes information about the race and the dogs, a map of the course, and a set of extending ideas.

9. Have your child make snow people. Give your child an assortment of different-size Styrofoam™ balls, glue, toothpicks, and construction paper (all available at variety and craft stores). Gather materials such as sticks, leaves, stones, and flowers to decorate the snow people. Use toothpicks to hold the balls together and glue to attach the decorations. Display the finished snow people in the living or family room.

RELATED CHILDREN'S BOOKS

Snowy Day by Caroline Feller Bauer
Katy and the Big Snow by Virginia Lee Burton
A Walk on a Snowy Night by Judy Delton
Snow Company by Marc Harshman
The First Snowfall by Anne F. Rockwell
The Big Snow by Berta and Elmer Hader
The Winter Bear by Ruth Craft
Life on Ice by Seymour Simon
The Snow by John Burningham
The Snow Book by Eva Knox Evans
Snow Bunny by Bubbi Katz
The Snow Parade by Barbara Brenner
Midnight Snowman by Caroline Bauer
Out of Doors in Winter by Clarence J. Hylander

The Story of Ferdinand
Munro Leaf
(New York: Viking, 1936)

STORY SUMMARY

Ferdinand is a bull who enjoys sitting under his favorite tree and smelling the flowers from the meadows. One day he is chosen for the bullfight in Madrid. However, all he does is sit and smell the flowers. Eventually, Ferdinand is sent back to his meadow.

DISCUSSION QUESTIONS

1. Why didn't Ferdinand like to play with the other bulls?

2. Why do you think Ferdinand did not want to fight?

3. If you were the author of this story, how would you change Ferdinand?

4. Do you think this story has a happy ending? Why or why not?

ACTIVITIES (Please choose any two activities.)

1. Invite your child to write or dictate a sequel to this story. What does Ferdinand do once he returns to the meadow? Does he have any more adventures?

2. Have your child write or dictate a story from Ferdinand's point of view, using the title "When I am Sitting under a Cork Tree."

3. Visit a local travel agent and obtain some brochures on Spain. Share these with your child and locate Spain on a map or globe of the world. Have your child plan an imaginary trip to Spain. How would he or she get there? What would be needed for the trip? How long would the trip take? How long would he or she wish to stay?

4. Ask your child to talk with various friends, relatives, and neighbors about their favorite sports. Encourage your child to keep a list of sports mentioned most often. What sports are not mentioned at all?

5. Divide a piece of paper into two sections. Ask your child to make a list of the things Ferdinand liked and another list of the things Ferdinand did not like. Which list is longer? Why?

6. Your child may enjoy other books by Munro Leaf, including *Wee Gillis, Gordon the Goat, Noodle,* and *Boo, Who Used to Be Scared of the Dark*.

RELATED CHILDREN'S BOOKS

Old Blue by Sibyl Hancock
Pistachio by Blair Lent
The Curious Cow by Esther K. Meeks
Daisy by Brian Wildsmith
The Story of Pancho and the Bull with the Crooked Tail by Berta Hoerner Hader
I Know What I Like by Norma Simon
Jasmine by Roger Duvoisin

Project for *The Story of Ferdinand*

DIRECTIONS

Have your child pretend that the two of you are traveling in another country (Spain, for example). Use the following postcard outlines to write a message home to the other members of the family describing what you are seeing (bulls, bullfights, etc.) and experiencing on your journey.

Tales of Oliver Pig

Jean Van Leeuwen
(New York: The Dial Press, 1979)

STORY SUMMARY

This book has five stories about Oliver, his younger sister, Amanda, and his mother and father. In the first story, Oliver and his mother make cookies on a rainy day. Then, there is a day when he refuses to share with Amanda, but he does get her to eat dinner when his parents can not. Another story tells of a special visit from Grandmother. Finally, there's a snowy day story and a tale of a special hide-and-seek game with Father.

DISCUSSION QUESTIONS

1. What do you like to do on a rainy day?

2. Why is it important to play fair with other people?

3. If you could, what would you most like to do in the snow?

4. How are pigs similar to humans? How are they different?

5. If you could tell the author to add one more story about Oliver, what would you want it to be about?

ACTIVITIES (Please choose any two activities.)

1. Make oatmeal cookies together using the following recipe.

1¼ cups margarine	1½ cups all-purpose flour
¾ cup firmly packed brown sugar	1 teaspoon baking soda
½ cup granulated sugar	1 teaspoon cinnamon
1 egg	¼ teaspoon nutmeg
1 teaspoon vanilla	3 cups uncooked oats

   Beat together margarine and sugars until light and fluffy. Beat in egg and vanilla. Combine flour, baking soda, and spices, and add to margarine mixture, mixing well. Stir in oats. Drop rounded teaspoonfuls of dough onto ungreased cookie sheets. Bake 8-9 minutes at 375°. Makes 4½ dozen cookies.

2. Ask your child to draw Oliver living on a farm instead of in a house. Discuss the differences between living in a house and on a farm (for a pig, that is).

3. Have your child write or dictate a story about another farm animal leaving the farm to live elsewhere. Why is the animal leaving and where is it going?

4. Ask your child to give you a summary of his or her favorite Oliver Pig story. What qualities does that story have that make it so good?

5. Provide your child with several paper bags to create some of the book characters using the bags as puppets. Retell a story while your child manipulates one or more of the puppets.

6. Talk with your child about how sometimes we all have a bad day. Have your child write or talk about a bad day he or she has had and what could have been done to make it better.

7. Children need to understand the importance of sharing. Talk with your child about his or her feelings about sharing. Then encourage your child to show something he or she is proud of, such as an original creation, a rare item, a favorite toy, etc. Talk with your child about how he or she would feel about sharing that item with a friend.

8. If possible, allow your child to interview a grandparent or an older relative. Your child could ask questions about life when that person was growing up and about activities in "the good old days." How do those activities compare with your child's regular activities?

RELATED CHILDREN'S BOOKS

How to Draw Farm Animals by Arthur Zaidenberg
Look at the Farm Animals by June Behrens
The True Book of Farm Animals by John Bryan Lewellen
Born in a Barn: Farm Animals and Their Young by Elizabeth Gemming and Klaus Gemming
Pigs at Christmas by Arlene Dubanevich
Amanda Pig and Her Big Brother Oliver by Jean Van Leeuwen
Oliver, Amanda and Grandmother by Jean Van Leeuwen
Pig Will and Pig Won't by Richard Scarry
Harvey the Foolish Pig by Dick Gackenbach

There's a Nightmare in My Closet

Mercer Mayer
(New York: Dial Books, 1968)

STORY SUMMARY

A little boy confronts the "nightmare" in his bedroom closet and discovers that it is not so scary after all. He tucks the nightmare into bed with him, and they both go to sleep.

DISCUSSION QUESTIONS

1. Have you ever had a nightmare? How did it make you feel?

2. Should we be afraid of the dark? Why or why not?

3. Do you think the boy in the story is brave? Why or why not?

4. Have you ever thought that there was something hiding in your closet? If so, what was it?

5. How would the story have changed if the nightmare in the story had not been afraid of the boy?

6. Why is it sometimes difficult to fall asleep at night?

7. What would you do if you heard a noise in your room at night?

8. Why do we think of scary things when it is dark?

ACTIVITIES (Please choose any two activities.)

1. Ask your child, "If you had a nightmare in your bedroom, what would it look like?" Have your child draw a picture of the nightmare, explain where it would hide, and write or tell about how he or she would handle it.

2. Have your child draw a diagram or take photographs of his or her room. Circle one or more likely places for a monster to dwell. Discuss the reasons for his or her selecting those locations.

3. Encourage your child to rewrite or retell the story from the nightmare's point of view. Discuss how the nightmare might feel as it waits in the closet, why it is in there, what it is looking for as it tiptoes across the bedroom, etc.

4. Read the story *There's an Alligator under My Bed* by Mercer Mayer (New York: Dial Books, 1987). The boy in the story is the same character that is in *There's a Nightmare in My Closet*. He is older now and has a new problem. Have your child make a list of similarities and differences between the two books. Identify the problem for each story and the steps the boy takes to solve his problem. Does he approach a problem differently now that he is older?

5. Share several poems from *Amazing Monsters: Verses to Thrill and Chill* by Robert Fisher (Boston: Faber & Faber, 1982). Have your child create his or her own amazing monster and draw a picture or write a poem about it.

6. Create monster tracks. Provide a large tray of damp soil and have your child press his or her hands, shoes, or other objects into the soil to create a version of a monster footprint. Pour plaster of paris (available at any hardware store) into the track. Allow it to dry. Ask your child to write an imaginary story about where the tracks were found and what type of monster made them.

7. Have your child write a sequel to the story—for example, "Another Nightmare in My Closet."

RELATED CHILDREN'S BOOKS

What's under My Bed? by James Stevenson
How to Get Rid of Bad Dreams by Nancy Hazbry and Roy Condy
Harry (the Monster) by Ann Cameron
There Was Nobody There by Barbara Bottner
Little Monster's Bedtime Book by Mercer Mayer
Little Monster's Neighborhood by Mercer Mayer
There's Something in My Attic by Mercer Mayer
You're the Scaredy Cat by Mercer Mayer
There's a Monster under My Bed by James Howe
Under the Bed by Michael Rosen
It Must Have Been the Wind by Barney Saltzberg
There's a Crocodile under My Bed! by Ingrid Schubert
The Beast in the Bathtub by Kathleen Stevens
Chasing the Goblins Away by Tobi Tobias
My Mama Says There Aren't Any Zombies, Ghosts, Vampires, Creatures, Demons, Monsters, Fiends, Goblins or Things by Judith Viorst
The Monster Bed by Jeane Willis
Timothy and the Night Noises by Jeffrey Dinardo
In the Middle of the Night by Aileen Fisher

The Three Bears
Paul Galdone
(New York: Seabury, 1972)

STORY SUMMARY

This is the traditional story of Goldilocks and the three bears. It details the adventures (or misadventures) of Goldilocks as she breaks into the house of the three bears. Delightful illustrations highlight this retelling.

DISCUSSION QUESTIONS

1. If you had been the little wee bear, how would you have felt about Goldilocks eating all of your porridge, breaking your chair, and messing up your bed?

2. What do you think the bears would have done to Goldilocks if she had not run away?

3. Do you think the three bears will leave their door unlocked the next time? Why?

4. What would you have done if you had found somebody strange sleeping in your bed?

5. Would you like to have Goldilocks as a friend? Why or why not?

ACTIVITIES (Please choose any two activities.)

1. Invite your child to create a sequel to this story—perhaps one titled "Goldilocks Returns." What adventures would Goldilocks have on the return visit?

2. Have your child pretend that there are three Goldilocks and one bear. How would the story change? Ask your child to dictate or write a new version of the tale.

3. Work with your child to make a simple identification card (similar to your driver's license) that could be used in case he or she ever got lost. You can go together to a local police station and talk with an officer about what to do if one gets lost.

4. Invite other family members to produce and put on a play about Goldilocks and the three bears using simple props (chairs, beds, bowls, etc.) and simple actions. If possible, videotape the play and show it to friends and neighbors.

5. Take your child to the local grocery store and try to identify the number of times the word *bear* shows up on products (e.g., bear cereal, bear cookies). Have your child make a list of various products that use the word *bear*.

RELATED CHILDREN'S BOOKS BY PAUL GALDONE

The Little Red Hen
The Three Billy Goats Gruff
Three Aesop Fox Fables
The Three Little Pigs
The Monkey and the Crocodile
Henny Penny
The Horse, the Fox, and the Lion

Project for *The Three Bears*

DIRECTIONS

Below is an imaginary letter Goldilocks might have written to an advice columnist. Read the letter to your child and work together to develop an appropriate response. Try to include two suggestions in the reply letter.

Dear Abby,

Everybody picks on me! Every time I go to visit one of the neighbors in the forest I always get chased away. In fact, I'm scared of the Grizzly family at the other side of the forest. What can I do so that the neighbors will invite me to their homes?

Sincerely,

Goldilocks

Your Response: _____

_____

_____

_____

_____

_____

_____

_____

_____

_____

_____

Two Bad Ants
Chris Van Allsburg
(Boston: Houghton Mifflin, 1988)

STORY SUMMARY

A group of ants sets out on a journey to get some delicious-tasting crystals for their queen. After several adventures, two ants discover that it is too dangerous to live outside the safety of their colony. They return to their home to discover the real treasures of life.

DISCUSSION QUESTIONS

1. What are some places ants can get into that we cannot?

2. What are some other things the ants could have found in the kitchen that would have made them want to stay?

3. What are some other things in a kitchen that could be dangerous to an ant?

ACTIVITIES (Please choose any two activities.)

1. Encourage your child to create a story describing the adventures of the ants in a different room, such as the bathroom, bedroom, or laundry room. Have your child tell the story from the ants' point of view.

2. Together collect some ants outdoors. Fill a jar with some loose soil and several ants (the jar should be filled half way). Place the jar in a warm, but not sunny, place and wrap a piece of black paper around the jar. Take the paper off once or twice a day to watch the ants. Discuss about any changes you see. The ants can be fed a solution of sugar water gently sprinkled over the soil. After about two weeks, be sure to return the ants outdoors.

3. Encourage your child to invent a story titled "A Day in the Life of an Ant."

4. Read the book *Ant Cities* by Arthur Dorros (New York: Harper & Row, 1987) to your child. Have your child compare the ant city to a people city. Work together to create a story similar to *Ant Cities* titled *People Cities*.

5. Put one or two ants on a sheet of graph paper. Measure the speed of the ants (how many squares covered in one minute). Conduct this experiment again with a drop of sugar water placed at one end of the paper. Do the ants move faster toward the sugar water?

RELATED CHILDREN'S BOOKS

"I Can't," Said the Ant by Polly Cameron
Never Say Ugh to a Bug by Norma Farber
The Ants Go Marching by Bernice Freschet
Ants Are Fun by Mildred Myrick
The Ant and the Elephant by Bill Peet

The Ugly Duckling

Hans Christian Andersen
(New York: Harcourt Brace Jovanovich, 1979)

STORY SUMMARY

This is the time-honored story of a swan who is misplaced into a nest of ducklings. Since he looks different from the ducklings, he is taunted and teased. Eventually, he leaves the nest to find his own kind.

DISCUSSION QUESTIONS

1. Do you think it is more important to be beautiful on the inside or on the outside?

2. Do you think the swan was treated fairly? Why?

3. How would it feel if nobody liked you?

4. How did the ending of the story make you feel?

5. What do you think would have happened if the swan had been unable to find his relatives?

ACTIVITIES (Please choose any two activities.)

1. Work with your child to make some paper-bag puppets of swans. Re-create a portion of the story using the puppets. Invite your child to create some original dialogue.

2. Work together to create a replica of a castle. Use milk cartons, cardboard boxes, shoe boxes, or any other kind of box to create a life-size replica of a castle. Invite other family members to help.

3. Talk with your child about how he or she felt after reading this story. Is there anything in the story that might apply to your child? How is the ugly duckling similar to your child? Has your child experienced anything similar to the adventures of the ugly duckling?

4. Take several photographs of your child over a period of several days. Post each photo on a separate piece of paper and ask your child to supply a caption or title for each one. Discuss some of the similarities as well as differences between the photos. Is it possible to look better one day in comparison to other days?

5. Bring out the family album and talk about some of your child's relatives, particularly when they were much younger. What physical or personality changes have taken place? In what ways do people change during their lifetime?

6. Is there a person, living or dead, whom your child admires? What qualities or characteristics does that person have that makes them admirable? Discuss the importance of being yourself rather than trying to be someone else.

RELATED CHILDREN'S BOOKS

A Story about Ping by Marjorie Flack
Angus and the Ducks by Marjorie Flack
Who Will Be My Friends? by Syd Hoff
Leo the Late Bloomer by Robert Kraus
Make Way for Ducklings by Robert McCloskey

Project for *The Ugly Duckling*

DIRECTIONS

Talk with your child about chickens, ducks, geese, and swans (check with your public or school librarian for books and illustrations on different kinds of birds). What are some of the differences? What are some of the similarities? Have your child draw an illustration of each in the spaces below.

DUCKS   **CHICKENS**

GEESE   **SWANS**

The Very Busy Spider
Eric Carle
(New York: Philomel, 1984)

STORY SUMMARY

A spider, blown across the barn yard, begins to spin a web. In the process, several of the farm animals stop to talk to the spider, but she is too busy to talk.

DISCUSSION QUESTIONS

1. What do you think of the spider?

2. Name some other places the spider could have spun her web? Why do you think she chose the fence?

3. Spiders must catch their food. How would you go about getting your food if you had to catch it?

4. Would you want to have the spider as a friend? Why or why not?

5. How would you feel if you were talking to someone and they were ignoring you? What would you do to gain their attention?

ACTIVITIES (Please choose any two activities.)

1. Work together to create a spider using pipe cleaners and Styrofoam balls painted black. Set up the spider in a web made from black thread. Display the spider and web in a corner of the living room.

2. Take several old sponges and cut each into the shape of a farm animal. Press each shape onto an ink pad (available at stationery and variety stores) and have your child create different farm scenes. Trees, barns, fences, and other background features can be drawn in with crayons.

3. Talk with your child about the reasons he or she feels it was important for the spider to finish spinning her web.

4. Read the story again, but this time have your child make the sounds of the animals as they appear in the story.

5. Talk with your child about proper manners to use when talking with someone. Work with your child to write a "guidebook" for kids on how they should behave when talking. Share the guide with other family members.

RELATED CHILDREN'S BOOKS

The Lady and the Spider by Faith McNulty
The Lives of Spiders by Dorothy Hinshaw Palens
Spider Silk by Augusta Golden
Spiders by Lillian Bason
Spiders Are Spinners by Teco Slagboon
On the Farm by Eugene Booth
Spiders by Dean Morris
Mimmy Spider's Work of Art by Sally Rippen

Project for *The Very Busy Spider*

DIRECTIONS

Ask your child to draw pictures in the boxes that could be used to illustrate each of the phrases below.

Places spiders live:

Things spiders eat:

Page 1 of a 2-page handout.

From *Involving Parents through Children's Literature: Grades 1-2*, 1992 • Libraries Unlimited, Inc. • P.O. Box 6633, Englewood, CO 80155-6633

What I like most (or least) about spiders:

The Very Hungry Caterpillar
Eric Carle
(New York: Crowell, 1976)

STORY SUMMARY

A caterpillar is born and goes through the week eating a variety of different foods. It finally spins a cocoon and eventually hatches into a beautiful butterfly.

DISCUSSION QUESTIONS

1. What part of the story did you enjoy most?

2. What else would you like to learn about caterpillars?

3. What are some of your favorite foods? What makes them so enjoyable?

4. What do you think the caterpillar was thinking about as it ate through all those foods?

5. If you could change into something else, what would it be?

ACTIVITIES (Please choose any two activities.)

1. Give your child several jelly beans, some nonpareils, some small pieces of pipe cleaners, and a toothpick. Your child can make a caterpillar by sticking the jelly beans on the toothpick, putting the pipe cleaners in the first jelly bean to resemble feelers, and gluing on the eyes (nonpareils).

2. Find a baby picture of your child. Glue the picture on a large sheet of paper and have your child use it as the head of a caterpillar, drawing the caterpillar's body on the paper. The illustration can be colored with crayons or watercolor paints. Be sure to display the picture.

3. Drape a sheet over a clothesline or between two chairs. Crawl inside with your child and retell the story. Discuss how it might feel to be inside a cocoon for an extended period of time.

4. Make up some word problems about the very hungry caterpillar. For example, if the caterpillar ate two apples on Wednesday and three peaches on Sunday, how much fruit did it eat in all? Or, if the caterpillar ate four apples on Tuesday, one watermelon on Thursday, and three pears on Saturday, how many pieces of fruit did it eat in all? Create other "problems" for other members of the family to solve.

5. Take your child for a walk to look for caterpillars. Caterpillars can usually be found on trees in warm weather. Collect a few in jars to observe later (place a twig with some leaves in the jar for food). Have your child observe and record how caterpillars act in their natural environment. Be sure to release the caterpillars after a few days.

6. Have your child write a sequel to *The Very Hungry Caterpillar* about the caterpillar's life as a butterfly.

7. Just for fun, work with your child to help the caterpillar go on a diet. Together write a weekly meal plan specifying how much the caterpillar should eat for breakfast, lunch, dinner, and snacks. The diet plan should also include the quantity, type, and nutritional value of the food.

RELATED CHILDREN'S BOOKS

Caterpillars by Dorothy Sterling
Caterpillars and How They Live by Robert M. McClung
A First Look at Caterpillars by Millicent Ellis Selsam
I Like Caterpillars by Gladys Conklin
The Pet in the Jar by Judy Stang
Scaly Wings: About Moths and Their Caterpillars by Ross E. Hutchins

Other Books by Eric Carle:
   Do You Want to Be My Friend?
   The Grouchy Ladybug
   Have You Seen My Cat?
   Honeybee and the Robber
   House for Hermit Crab
   Mixed-Up Chameleon
   1,2,3 to the Zoo
   Rooster's Off to See the World
   Secret Birthday Message
   Tiny Seed
   The Very Busy Spider

Where the Wild Things Are

Maurice Sendak
(New York: Harper & Row, 1963)

STORY SUMMARY

A small boy, sent to bed without his supper, imagines himself to be the master of all the wild things. The smell of his dinner being brought to his room brings him back to reality.

DISCUSSION QUESTIONS

1. Why do you think Max was sent to bed without supper?

2. Would you like to visit the wild things? Why?

3. Why do you think Max became king of all the wild things?

4. Do you think Max will ever go back to visit the wild things?

5. What do you think your friends would enjoy most about this book?

ACTIVITIES (Please choose any two activities.)

1. Have your child pretend to be a reporter who has just spotted the wild things for the very first time. Have him or her write or dictate a newspaper-style article that includes who, what, and where. For example, "A mysterious, 10-foot-tall creature called 'Wild Thing' was spotted yesterday by a group of vacationing kids in the jungle of Forty Winks."

2. Together create a scary costume catalog. Ask your child to draw several examples of scary costumes. Look through some old magazines for pictures of outfits that could be used as part of a scary costume. Put together a catalog that offers a variety of costumes (including sizes, prices, etc.) that could be used in the Land of the Wild Things.

3. Ask your child to think of all the places a monster or nightmare could hide in his or her room and to draw up a plan for "monster-proofing" the bedroom. Compile the ideas into a how-to manual for other kids who may worry about monsters at night.

4. Your child may enjoy reading other books by Maurice Sendak, including *In the Night Kitchen, Chicken Soup with Rice, Outside Over There*, and *Rosie and Michael.*

5. Ask your child to lie down on a large sheet of newsprint. Trace an outline of your child's body on the paper. Provide your child with crayons and paints to turn the outline into a wild thing. Post the finished drawing.

RELATED CHILDREN'S BOOKS

The Night Flight by Joanne Ryder
Daddy Is a Monster ... Sometimes by John Steptoe
When I'm Sleepy by Jane R. Howard
A Monster in the Mailbox by Sheila Gordon
My Mama Says There Aren't Any Zombies, Ghosts, Vampires, Creatures, Demons, Monsters, Fiends, Goblins, or Things by Judith Viorst

Project for *Where the Wild Things Are*

DIRECTIONS

Here are several forms of transportation:

horse   car   boat   bicycle   train   airplane

Ask your child to select any three of the above and write them in the boxes on the left side of the chart below. Then have your child pretend that he or she is taking a one-week trip to the Land of the Wild Things using the first form of transportation. Ask your child to create and describe the imaginary places in the Land of the Wild Things he or she would visit and what he or she would see there. Repeat for the other two forms of transportation. Encourage your child to use as much imagination as possible. There are no right or wrong answers.

Form of transportation	Places I would go	What I would see

Appendix
Supplementary Materials for Parents

LETTER 1

Dear Parents:

One of the questions parents frequently ask teachers is, "What are some appropriate books for my child to read?" As you may imagine, when children are encouraged to read good literature, and are supported in those efforts, reading skills develop dramatically. As part of our effort to help you help your child experience good books, we will be sending you specially prepared activity pages. Each activity page identifies a specific children's book recommended for your child's grade level. Included is a brief summary of the book, some discussion questions for you and your child to share, a selection of exciting activities for you and your child to do together, and, in some cases, a separate project sheet for your child to work on.

Each time you receive one of the activity pages please obtain a copy of the recommended book. You can do this through your local public library or the school library; or you can borrow one from a friend or neighbor, purchase a copy at a local bookstore, or obtain a copy from your home library. Plan to read the book with your child over the course of one or more days. You may elect to read the book aloud to your child, your child may wish to read the book by himself or herself, or your child may want to read the book out loud to you. It is important that you set aside some time each day for you and your child to read together.

After reading the book, take some time to share some of the suggested questions with your child. These questions are designed to help your child think carefully about the book and what that book means to him or her, not to "test" your child on what he or she remembers about the book. Of course, you and your child are encouraged to think of other questions to talk about together.

Each page contains a variety of extending activities related to the book for you and your child to do together. It is not important that you complete all the activities. Share the suggestions with your child and decide together on two or three you would enjoy working on together. Each activity has been designed to help your child gain a fuller appreciation of the book and to offer some exciting learning opportunities. Most of the activity materials can be easily found at home or inexpensively purchased at a nearby hardware, stationery, or variety store.

The time you spend with your child in reading these books and doing the suggested activities should be relaxed, comfortable, and supportive. By working together in an encouraging way you will be helping your child discover the wonder and excitement of good literature while also promoting his or her reading development. Reading the suggested books and participating in the suggested activities on a regular basis can be an important part of your child's growth in reading this year.

I am looking forward to working with you this year. I hope you will feel free to contact me at any time if I can provide you with any additional information or assistance.

Sincerely,

From *Involving Parents through Children's Literature: Grades 1-2,* 1992 • Libraries Unlimited, Inc. • P.O. Box 6633, Englewood, CO 80155-6633

LETTER 2

Dear Parents:

Many parents ask for additional resources to help their children grow and learn in reading. The following books, booklets, and brochures are highly recommended and will provide you with a wealth of ideas on how you can help your child become a more successful reader. Your local public library should have these books available for you to check out. Any good-sized bookstore will also have one or more of the books in stock or can order them for you.

Books

Clinard, Linda. *The Reading Triangle*. Belmont, CA: David S. Lake, 1985.
This book presents practical and useful ideas on how parents can work together with teachers to establish a strong reading environment at home.

Copperman, Paul. *Taking Books to Heart*. Reading, MA: Addison-Wesley, 1986.
This book provides a thorough overview of reading programs in schools and also offers an annotated bibliography of read-aloud fiction for children through fourth grade.

Graves, Ruth, ed. *The RIF Guide to Encouraging Young Readers*. New York: Doubleday, 1987.
This book includes an extensive list of recommended books for children through sixth grade. In addition, there is a wealth of reading activities parents and children can share together.

Kaye, Peggy. *Games for Reading*. New York: Pantheon, 1984.
Contains many interesting and educational games designed to stimulate children's reading growth and development. All the suggestions can be easily incorporated into any family's daily activities.

Kimmel, Margaret, and Elizabeth Segal. *For Reading Out Loud: A Guide to Sharing Books with Children*. New York: Delacorte, 1988.
More than 300 recommended read-aloud titles are included in this book for parents of children from preschool to sixth grade. Lots of tips for reading with and to children of all ages are included.

Kobrin, Beverly. *Eye Openers: How to Choose and Use Children's Books about Real People, Places, and Things*. New York: Viking, 1988.
This book has an extensive annotated bibliography of nonfiction books for children of all ages. Includes suggested activities parents and children can use with selected books.

Landsberg, Michele. *Reading for the Love of It: Best Books for Young Readers*. New York: Prentice-Hall, 1986.
More than 400 books specifically for the older child and teenager are described in this book. Also discussed are the uses of literature at home and school.

From *Involving Parents through Children's Literature: Grades 1-2*, 1992 • Libraries Unlimited, Inc. • P.O. Box 6633, Englewood, CO 80155-6633

Larrick, Nancy. *Parent's Guide to Children's Reading*. 5th ed. New York: Bantam, 1982.

This classic book provides a wealth of information for parents on how to stimulate and maintain the reading habit. Lists of suggested books are also provided.

Lipson, Eden. *The New York Times Parent's Guide to the Best Books for Children*. New York: Times Books, 1988.

More than 1,000 books for children of all ages are cataloged and described in this engaging booklist. There is something for everyone here.

Oppenheim, Joanne, Barbara Brenner, and Betty Boegehold. *Choosing Books for Kids*. New York: Ballantine, 1986.

A thorough and complete annotation of hundreds of books organized by age level and book topics. Includes suggestions on the importance of reading with children.

Reed, Arthea J. S. *Comics to Classics*. Newark, DE: International Reading Association, 1988.

This book provides parents with valuable insights on helping teens and preteens gain and retain the reading habit. Includes ideas and techniques parents can use to help draw teens into reading, and ideas on locating appropriate books.

Taylor, Barbara M., and Dianne L. Monson. *Reading Together: Helping Children Get a Good Start in Reading*. Glenview, IL: Scott, Foresman, 1991.

This book is a collection of stimulating activities specifically designed for busy parents to share with their children in short periods of time. Includes a guide to the wide variety of reading materials available for children.

Trelease, Jim. *The New Read-Aloud Handbook*. New York: Penguin, 1989.

This handbook tells parents why and how to read aloud to their children and what parents can do to make reading a meaningful part of their child's life. Includes a list of hundreds of recommended books for all ages.

Booklets

The following booklets answer questions parents often ask about the education of their children. Each one is filled with sound, practical, and useful advice on helping you help your child grow and learn. They are published by the International Reading Association and can be purchased for $1.75 (each). Write to the International Reading Association (800 Barksdale Road, P.O. Box 8139, Newark, DE 19714-8139).

Baghban, Marcia. *You Can Help Your Young Child with Writing* (No. 160), 1989.

Beverstock, Caroline. *Your Child's Vision Is Important* (No. 167), 1990.

Glazer, Susan Mandel. *Creating Readers and Writers* (No. 165), 1990.

Grinnell, Paula C. *How Can I Prepare My Young Child for Reading?* (No. 163), 1989.

Myers, Jamie. *You Can Encourage Your High School Students to Read* (No. 162), 1989.

Roser, Nancy L. *Helping Your Child Become a Reader* (No. 161), 1989.

Shefelbine, John. *Encouraging Your Junior High Student to Read* (No. 168), 1991.

Silvern, Steven, and Linda Silvern. *Beginning Literacy and Your Child* (No. 164), 1990.

Brochures

The following brochures offer a variety of ideas and tips on how you can help your child become the best student possible. They are available *free of charge* from the International Reading Association (800 Barksdale Road, P.O. Box 8139, Newark, DE 19714-8139). To order one to three brochures send a self-addressed, stamped envelope with first class postage for 1 ounce. Orders for four to seven brochures should be accompanied by a self-addressed, stamped envelope with first-class postage for 2 ounces. Requests for eight to ten titles require first-class postage for 3 ounces.

- Your Home Is Your Child's First School**

- You Can Encourage Your Child to Read**

- Good Books Make Reading Fun for Your Child*

- Summer Reading Is Important*

- You Can Use Television to Stimulate Your Child's Reading Habits**

- Studying: A Key to Success ... Ways Parents Can Help

- You Can Help Your Child in Reading by Using the Newspaper*

- Eating Well Can Help Your Child Learn Better

- You Can Prepare Your Child for Reading Tests

- You Can Help Your Child Connect Reading to Writing

---

* Also available in French

** Also available in French and Spanish

LETTER 3

Dear Parents:

    The following 99 books are highly recommended for students in first and second grades. These books have been selected on the basis of their appropriateness to children's interests and represent a wide range of award-winning and frequently cited books for this age level. Your local public library, your child's school library, or any local bookstore will have these books available for you.

Ackerman, Karen. *Song and Dance Man*. New York: Knopf, 1988.

Aliki. *Digging up Dinosaurs*. New York: Crowell, 1988.

_____. *We Are Best Friends*. New York: Greenwillow, 1982.

Allard, Harry. *The Stupids Step Out*. Boston: Houghton Mifflin, 1974.

Asch, Frank. *Happy Birthday, Moon!* New York: Prentice-Hall, 1982.

Balian, Lorna. *The Aminal*. New York: Abingdon, 1972.

Bang, Molly. *The Paper Crane*. New York: Greenwillow, 1985.

_____. *Ten, Nine, Eight*. New York: Greenwillow, 1983.

Barrett, Judi. *Animals Should Definitely Not Wear Clothing*. New York: Atheneum, 1970.

Bate, Lucy. *Little Rabbit's Loose Tooth*. New York: Crown, 1975.

Bemelmans, Ludwig. *Madeline*. New York: Viking, 1939.

Blume, Judy. *The Pain and the Great One*. New York: Bradbury Press, 1984.

Bunting, Eve. *The Wednesday Surprise*. New York: Clarion, 1989.

Burton, Virginia Lee. *Katy and the Big Snow*. Boston: Houghton Mifflin, 1943.

Carrick, Carol. *Sleep Out*. New York: Clarion, 1973.

Ciardi, John. *You Read to Me, I'll Read to You*. New York: Lippincott, 1962.

Clement, Claude. *The Painter and the Wild Swans*. New York: Dial Press, 1986.

Cohen, Miriam. *Will I Have a Friend?* New York: Macmillan, 1987.

From *Involving Parents through Children's Literature: Grades 1-2*, 1992 • Libraries Unlimited, Inc. • P.O. Box 6633, Englewood, CO 80155-6633

79

Coville, Bruce, and Katherine Coville. *Sarah's Unicorn*. New York: Lippincott, 1979.

Crowe, Robert L. *Tyler Toad and the Thunder*. New York: Dutton, 1980.

Dayrell, Elphinstone. *Why the Sun and the Moon Live in the Sky*. Boston: Houghton Mifflin, 1968.

dePaola, Tomie. *Strega Nona*. New York: Prentice-Hall, 1975.

Du Bois, William Pene. *Lion*. New York: Viking, 1957.

Duvoisin, Roger. *Petunia*. New York: Knopf, 1950.

Flora, James. *The Great Green Turkey Creek Monster*. New York: Atheneum, 1976.

Fowles, John. *Cinderella*. Boston: Little, Brown, 1976.

Freeman, Don. *Dandelion*. New York: Viking, 1964.

Galdone, Paul. *The Three Billy Goats Gruff*. New York: Clarion, 1973.

Geringer, Laura. *A Three Hat Day*. New York: Harper & Row, 1985.

Gibbons, Gail. *Department Store*. New York: Crowell, 1984.

Goble, Paul. *Death of the Iron Horse*. New York: Bradbury Press, 1987.

Grifalconi, Ann. *The Village of Round and Square Houses*. Boston: Little, Brown, 1986.

Haas, Irene. *The Maggie B*. New York: Atheneum, 1975.

Hall, Donald. *Ox-Cart Man*. New York: Viking, 1979.

Hest, Amy. *The Purple Coat*. New York: Four Winds, 1986.

Hines, Anna Grossnickle. *Sky All Around*. New York: Clarion, 1989.

Houston, Gloria. *The Year of the Perfect Christmas Tree: An Appalachian Story*. New York: Dial Press, 1988.

Jeschke, Susan. *Perfect the Pig*. New York: Holt, Rinehart & Winston, 1981.

Jonas, Ann. *Round Trip*. New York: Greenwillow, 1983.

Keats, Ezra Jack. *Peter's Chair*. New York: Harper & Row, 1967.

Kellogg, Steven. *The Island of the Skog*. New York: Dial Books, 1973.

_____. *Pecos Bill*. New York: Morrow, 1986.

_____. *A Rose for Pinkerton*. New York: Dial Press, 1981.

Krauss, Ruth. *The Carrot Seed*. New York: Harper & Row, 1945.

Levy, Elizabeth. *Nice Little Girls*. New York: Delacorte, 1978.

Lewin, Hugh. *Jafta*. Minneapolis: Carolrhoda, 1983.

Lionni, Leo. *Alexander and the Wind-Up Mouse*. New York: Pantheon, 1969.

_____. *Frederick*. New York: Pantheon, 1966.

Lobel, Arnold. *Frog and Toad Together*. New York: Harper & Row, 1971.

_____. *Mouse Soup*. New York: Harper & Row, 1977.

_____. *On Market Street*. New York: Greenwillow, 1981.

Locker, Thomas. *The Mare on the Hill*. New York: Dial Press, 1985.

MacLachlan, Patricia. *Through Grandpa's Eyes*. New York: Harper & Row, 1980.

McDermott, Gerald. *Anansi the Spider: A Tale from the Ashanti*. New York: Holt, 1972.

McGovern, Ann. *Stone Soup*. New York: Scholastic, 1986.

McKissack, Patricia. *Mirandy and Brother Wind*. New York: Knopf, 1988.

Miller, Alice. *Mousekin's Fables*. New York: Prentice-Hall, 1982.

Monjo, F. N. *The Drinking Gourd*. New York: Harper & Row, 1970.

Ness, Evaline. *Sam, Bangs, and Moonshine*. New York: Henry Holt, 1966.

Numeroff, Laura Joffe. *If You Give a Mouse a Cookie*. New York: Harper & Row, 1985.

Ormondroyd, Edward. *Broderick*. Boston: Houghton Mifflin, 1984.

Parish, Peggy. *Amelia Bedelia*. New York: Harper & Row, 1963.

Patterson, Francine. *Koko's Kitten*. New York: Scholastic, 1985.

Peet, Bill. *Big Bad Bruce*. Boston: Houghton Mifflin, 1977.

Pinkwater, Daniel Manus. *The Big Orange Splot*. New York: Scholastic, 1981.

Plume, Ilse. *The Bremen Town Musicians* (retold from the Brothers Grimm). New York: Doubleday, 1980.

Politi, Leo. *Song of the Swallows*. New York: Scribner's, 1949.

Potter, Beatrix. *The Complete Adventures of Peter Rabbit*. New York: Warne, 1987.

Prelutsky, Jack. *The Baby Uggs Are Hatching*. New York: Greenwillow, 1982.

———. *Read-Aloud Rhymes for the Very Young*. New York: Knopf, 1986.

Rylant, Cynthia. *Night in the Country*. New York: Bradbury Press, 1986.

———. *The Relatives Came*. New York: Bradbury Press, 1985.

Schwartz, Amy. *Bea and Mr. Jones*. New York: Bradbury Press, 1982.

Schwartz, David. *How Much Is a Million?* New York: Lothrop, Lee & Shepard Books, 1985.

Sharmat, Marjorie. *A Big Fat Enormous Lie*. New York: Dutton, 1978.

Shute, Linda. *Momotaro, the Peach Boy*. New York: Lothrop, Lee & Shepard Books, 1986.

Silverstein, Shel. *The Giving Tree*. New York: Harper & Row, 1964.

Slobodkina, Esphyr. *Caps for Sale*. New York: Harper & Row, 1947.

Snyder, Dianne. *The Boy of the Three-Year Nap*. Boston: Houghton Mifflin, 1988.

Steig, William. *Amos and Boris*. New York: Farrar, Straus, & Giroux, 1971.

Steiner, Barbara. *The Whale Brother*. New York: Walker, 1988.

Turkle, Brinton. *Thy Friend, Obadiah*. New York: Viking, 1969.

Udry, Janice May. *A Tree Is Nice*. New York: Harper & Row, 1956.

———. *What Mary Jo Shared*. New York: Albert Whitman, 1966.

Van Allsburg, Chris. *Jumanji*. Boston: Houghton Mifflin, 1981.

Viorst, Judith. *Alexander, Who Used to Be Rich Last Sunday*. New York: Atheneum, 1978.

_____. *I'll Fix Anthony*. New York: Harper & Row, 1969.

Waber, Bernard. *An Anteater Named Arthur*. Boston: Houghton Mifflin, 1967.

_____. *The House on East 88th Street*. Boston: Houghton Mifflin, 1962.

_____. *Lovable Lyle*. Boston: Houghton Mifflin, 1969.

Wadsworth, Olive. *Over in the Meadow: A Counting-Out Rhyme*. New York: Viking, 1985.

Ward, Lynd. *The Biggest Bear*. Boston: Houghton Mifflin, 1952.

Weiss, Nicki. *Princess Pearl*. New York: Greenwillow, 1986.

Yashima, Taro. *Crow Boy*. New York: Viking, 1955.

Yolen, Jane. *Owl Moon*. New York: Philomel, 1987.

Yorinks, Arthur. *Hey, Al*. New York: Farrar, Straus, & Giroux, 1986.

Zelinsky, Paul. *Rumpelstiltskin* (retold from the Brothers Grimm). New York: Dutton, 1986.

Zemach, Margot. *It Could Always Be Worse*. New York: Farrar, Straus, & Giroux, 1976.

Zolotow, Charlotte. *The Quarreling Book*. New York: Harper & Row, 1963.

Index

About the Author

Anthony D. Fredericks

Anthony D. Fredericks received his bachelor of arts degree in history from the University of Arizona, his master's degree in reading from Kutztown State College in Pennsylvania, and his doctor of education degree in reading from Lehigh University.

Tony has been a classroom teacher and reading specialist in public and private schools for more than fifteen years. He is a frequent presenter and storyteller at conferences, reading councils, schools and inservice meetings throughout the United States and Canada. The author or coauthor of more than two hundred articles and nineteen books, he has written for *The Reading Teacher*, *Reading Today*, and *Teaching K-8*. He is recipient of many education awards, including the Innovative Teaching Award from the Pennsylvania State Education Association.

Tony currently resides in Glen Rock, Pennsylvania, with his wife, Phyllis, two children, Rebecca and Jonathan, and four cats. He is an Assistant Professor of Education at York College, York, Pennsylvania, where he teaches methods courses in reading, language arts, science, and social studies.